Alternatives in Education: Schools and Programs

Curriculum Improvement Series

ALBERT I. OLIVER
University of Pennsylvania
Consulting Editor

Alternatives in Education: Schools and Programs

Allan A. Glatthorn
University of Pennsylvania

Dodd, Mead & Company
New York   1975

Contents

Tables

Preface

Until recently the selection of a school was a simple problem for contemporary American students and their parents. Unless you were wealthy and could afford a private school, or were Roman Catholic and preferred the parochial school, the chances are that you attended the community public school. In almost every American community there was only one public school system, one "comprehensive" public high school which prided itself on including all the young people of that community.

That picture has changed during the past ten years. All across the country small alternative schools have opened, providing educational choices to young people and their parents. Although reliable figures are very hard to come by in a movement that changes so rapidly, some observers held that as of 1974, there were upward of 2,000 schools that could be considered significantly different and available by choice.

In a certain sense, of course, the alternative school movement is simply a return to an early American model of schooling. As Sally Wertheim points out in her excellent historical review: "Alternative schools have been part of the American educational experience since schooling began in America in the seventeenth century. . . . Public schools, as we know them today, did not exist; rather people could choose the type of education they preferred from among many alternatives. The forms they developed included the very formal Latin Grammar

Schools; the more practical academies, which grew up later as a response to the classical training; the simplistic dame schools; moving schools in the South, which met the needs of an agrarian community; town schools; and such informal arrangements as tutors. Apprenticeship was also available to the less affluent and was an important form of education." ("Alternative Schools in Greater Cleveland," Sally H. Wertheim, Cleveland, Jennings Foundation, 1973, pp. 3–4.)

However, the need for a rapidly expanding nation to assimilate diverse ethnic groups gave rise to the "common school" movement of the nineteenth century and brought a temporary halt to the spread of educational pluralism. Except for the schools that were part of the utopian community movement of that century and for the parochial schools that were developing as a reaction against Protestant establishmentarianism, students and their parents had little choice of schools. It was not until the early part of this century that the resurgence of American educational pluralism began.

In the early decades of this century, two important educational theories strongly influenced first private schools and then public schools: the Montessori movement and Progressive education. The schools shaped by these two theories might be termed the first "alternative schools" of the contemporary era. Let us examine each of these briefly.

Although Maria Montessori opened her first Children's House in Italy in 1907, it wasn't until five years later that translations of her pedagogical works inspired Anne George to open the first United States Montessori school in Tarrytown, New York. Shortly thereafter several independent public and parochial schools were adopting the Montessori approach in their primary grades. Featuring a highly structured and stimuli-rich environment, the schools achieved significant success in helping young children develop autonomy and self-direction. While the child had real freedom of movement and the freedom to determine at any given time which of several learning activities he or she wanted to pursue, the freedom was exercised within the context of a highly structured learning environment which did not leave learning to chance. Unfortunately, American educators of the day did not recognize the great potential of the Montessori schools, and the movement failed to make a significant impact until its resurgence in the sixties, when Montessori schools became one model for alternative school people who were looking for prototypes.

A different approach to freedom for the child was typically found in the schools operated by the Progressive educators, who had been much influenced by the child-centered theories of men like John Dewey and Harold Rugg. Schools like the Children's School (later the Walden School), the Dalton School, and the Oak Lane Country Day School placed much more stress on the child's emerging interests as a primary factor in the development of curriculum, rather than developing that curriculum in advance and letting the child's interests determine only when he or she would work on a piece of it. There was, at least in practice, much less concern for structure and more concern for the spontaneous interchange between pupils and teachers. Despite the decline of the Progressive education movement in the 1940s and 1950s, these small Progressive schools were able to survive, providing at the elementary level, at least, a viable alternative to the conventional public schools.

But alternatives at the secondary level were almost nonexistent. While there were several public secondary schools experimenting with Progressive ideas in the 1930s and 1940s, they did not seem sufficiently different in their overall structures from the rest of the secondary schools to be called alternatives. There really was no choice: if you lived in Winnetka, Illinois, you attended the Winnetka schools and took part —perhaps unwillingly—in the Winnetka experiment.

This monolithic nature of the public school system was reinforced, curiously, by two widespread innovations of the period from 1955 to 1965. The first was the curriculum reform movement of the post-Sputnik era. Such "teacher-proof" curricula as PSSC physics, BSCS biology, SMSG mathematics, Project English, and Project Social Studies gave perhaps unwitting support to the notion that there was some ideal curriculum for all students and some best way to teach; the goal was academic rigor, not alternatives.

The second innovation which seemed to support the idea of a single comprehensive school was the set of scheduling and staffing approaches formulated and advocated by J. Lloyd Trump and others. The ideas of modular scheduling, team teaching, and flexible group instruction seemed effective for many students and teachers, and they were touted as an ideal solution for everyone. And the energies of creative school administrators and teachers were therefore devoted to trying to make that single set of innovations work effectively for all. Clearly, this was an impossible goal. Consequently, the "innovative" schools of the sixties were often as beset with problems as the "conventional" schools.

The period of the late sixties, then, was a time ripe for radical change. The curriculum reform movement had run out of steam. The innovations in scheduling and staffing were proving to be only superficial tinkering. And there was acute dissatisfaction with all the public schools. This dissatisfaction was most keenly sensed by militant blacks (and their white sympathizers) and by the radicals of the New Left. Each of these groups responded by opening their own schools, and these schools were the progenitors of the public alternatives that followed.

The response of militant blacks and their white supporters was to open so-called freedom schools. Convinced that the public schools were an instrument of an oppressive and racist society, these community activists opened storefront schools that emphasized black culture and basic skills. At the high school level, such community-based schools took on the additional challenge of enlisting school dropouts off the street corner and preparing them for college. Harlem Prep of New York and CAM Academy of Chicago were two highly successful freedom schools with a strong college-preparatory orientation. In all cases these freedom schools operated outside the system, drawing financial support from foundations and committed individuals.

Concurrent with the opening of the freedom schools was the development of the free school movement. Typically, such schools were opened by young radical whites of the New Left, who were convinced that the public school establishment was a tainted part of a sick society. Strongly influenced by a Freudian view of human nature and a Marxist view of society, these radical leaders opened small schools which most often were characterized by close, nonauthoritarian relationships between pupil and teacher and a politicalized curriculum which focused on the ills of a capitalistic society.

This free school movement had a rapid growth and instant notoriety. According to Allen Graubard, the early free schools, which by 1967 numbered no more than thirty, included some Progressive schools founded during the Progressive education movement, some Summerhillian schools, such as Lewis-Wadhams in Westport, New York, and some black community schools, like the Roxbury Community School in Boston. His study indicated that by 1971–72, free schools numbered well over 200 (Allen Graubard, *Free the Children*, New York: Random House, 1972). Even though small in numbers, however, the free schools were perhaps fortunate in that they were often led by articulate people, who knew how to tell their story and were successful in capturing the attention of media journalists looking for news about the counter-culture. So the late sixties saw a flood of articles and books about utopian free schools, where all learning was fun and all politics radical.

Undoubtedly, this success of the free school movement gave real encouragement to public school educators who were acutely dissatisfied with the "joyless" schools so often damned by fashionable critics like Charles Silberman. In another age these educators would have turned to one more "innovation" installed on a mass scale. However, with models of Montessori, storefront, and commune schools all around them, these early developers of public alternatives chose instead the free school model. While there is dispute about the first "true" public alternative school, certainly one of the most publicized of the early public alternatives was the Parkway Program in Philadelphia, which has its own interesting history. Late in 1968, Clifford Brenner, then an assistant to Mayor Richardson Dilworth, was concerned about finding money to build new schools when he realized that such available facilities as the art museum and the Franklin Institue of Science could be used for schooling. He sold the idea of a school that would use all the resources of the city to Mayor Dilworth and to Mark Shedd, then superintendent of schools. But it was John Bremer, the first director, who transformed the notion of a "school without walls" into a very exciting learning community. And it was Parkway that pointed the way for all those that followed—that showed that smallness could be cost-efficient, that proved that the school–community dichotomy was a false one, and that broke new ground in developing democratic structures for governance.

Metro in Chicago followed shortly thereafter, and soon every major city had its special kind of "Parkway" school, where the emphasis was on making effective use of community resources. But shortly, as with any burgeoning movement, this single type of alternative—the school without walls—was supplemented with a wide variety of alternative secondary schools.

Where do we stand today insofar as this movement is concerned? There is some tentative evidence that the free school movement is losing its steam. The quietism of the early seventies, the disenchantment of the radical activists, and the press of inflation on disposable income all mean that earlier projections of a widespread "free school revolution" were unreasonably idealistic. Allen Graubard, for example, certainly one of the free school movement's strongest supporters, concludes his own work with a somewhat pessimistic view of the movement's future.

Conversely, the spread of educational alternatives inside the system seems to be growing, despite the attacks of both conservative and radical critics. In almost every major community, parents and educators are either operating or planning to open some kind of alternative school or program. And their concern now is not to debate the theory or argue the merits but to learn how to establish alternatives.

This work attempts to respond specifically to that last concern. It is not concerned with the politics of free schools or the history of alternative education or the theory of radical reform. It is concerned instead with the strategies for planning, implementing, and evaluating all types of educational alternatives. And it is addressed to all those—administrators, teachers, parents, and students—who believe that the system is worth perpetuating and that alternatives can strengthen that system.

Many colleagues have been most helpful throughout the development of this work. Albert Oliver motivated me to begin writing it and was patient through many delays; Bruce Cooper was extremely helpful in showing me how weak an early version was and in suggesting ways to improve it; Sally Wertheim generously shared the results of her own research; Steven Selden challenged me to look beyond and behind my liberal biases; Arthur Hyde provided me with some important insights about curriculum; Carol Polzer helped with some important information retrieval; Elizabeth Stiles tended the store while I played author; and Jane Christensen helped me find a focus. But in the last analysis, it is my own work; I accept responsibility for its errors and admit its subjectivity.

I am also indebted, of course, to all those alternative schools that so generously shared their materials. The informality, candor, and lack of pretense reflected in most of those materials bode well for alternative education. Two creative practitioners in the field—and good friends—have been especially helpful: Patrick Pietrovito from Alternative West and Leonard Finkelstein, director of Philadelphia's Alternative Programs Office.

And, of course, like every compulsive author, I am indebted to the members of my family, who were patient and forbearing during the difficult gestation period.

I would like to conclude with a special acknowledgment to my colleagues at Abington North Campus and the Alternative Schools Project, who were so patient with my mistakes, so tolerant of my liberal notions, and so unflagging in their attempts to make my ideas work. I learned more from them than they ever realized.

ALLAN A. GLATTHORN

CHAPTER ONE

The Need for Alternatives: Opening Up the Options

How do we change the schools of the seventies?

That question is the central concern of this book. The author would argue that it is at the same time both a very important question and a very complicated one.

Its importance seems easily established. Education has become one of the central concerns of the American public. The impact of schooling on the daily life of the young is clear to any parent or student. And all constituents—educators, students, and parents—must be concerned with the short-term planning that should inform day-to-day decision making.

The complexity of the question perhaps needs a stronger defense, for at first glance the question seems simple enough. It does not ask the reader to fantasize about the year 2000, but to think about the short-term future. And it does not challenge the reader to think of education in its broadest sense, but to assume the continued importance of schooling. On the surface, the question seems so simple that the answers are obvious to those who offer their own panaceas—open education, career schools, basic skills laboratories, or whatever.

But the author would contend that the question is more complex and that no easy answers will suffice.

The complexity of the question stems primarily from the presence of strong countervailing tendencies in our society. In other times the drift seemed clear enough, even to those caught in the flow. One could sense the mood of a period: the fifties were placid and quiet; the sixties, disturbed and tumultuous. But of our own times, one is hard put to know the prevailing tides, and any wise educator will be sensitive to the ambiguities of the present situation, ambiguities that result from the uncertain drift of both conservative and liberal forces at work.

The conservative forces seem surprisingly strong in an era known as a time of change. The energy crisis forces us to reexamine a consumption-oriented life-style and makes past ways seem desirable, not simply quaint. Continuing inflation makes us all anxious about the amount of disposable income available to us, and this anxiety translates into demands for school "accountability." The power of teachers' unions and associations, while not the reactionary force that critics would suggest, serves as a brake on any precipitous change that would eliminate jobs or restrict the authority of the classroom teacher. The oversupply of teachers results in reduced turnover and decreased mobility, and an entrenched professional is not typically an active change agent. And an understandable concern about teen-age violence and vandalism becomes at its worst a desire for punitive control.

There are, however, equally strong tendencies moving in a liberal direction. Although the youth cult has not greened us all as Charles A. Reich (1970) foolishly predicted, the counterculture has made innovation fashionable. Teacher salary schedules, built to reward only the very experienced teachers, have forced school administrators to hire only the young and inexperienced to fill vacancies, and the college graduates now entering school classrooms as teachers were formed in a more radical age. And the children and young people themselves, seemingly without a past and oblivious to any tradition, call insistently for more change.

So there is no clear pattern for our times. One could predict that some historian of the future, looking back on the first half of this decade, would characterize these years as a time of drift and confusion. So neither the conservative educators, hoping for a reactionary backlash, nor the liberals, anticipating the greening of America, will find that they are moving with a strong tide.

Given this uncertainty, it seems, then, that any reasonable answer to that question of short-term change must emerge from a systematic examination of two related issues. The first is a question of necessity: what forces at work in the present will inevitably shape the choices we make? The second is a question of freedom: what choices *should* we make in those areas where options are possible?

The first force at work is a conservative force: the permanence of the conventional school. Despite the dire predictions of Ivan Illich (1971) and others, the school as we know it will continue to be an important institution in our society, for it meets critical needs of the society, the teacher, the parent, and the student. As Robert Dreeben (1968) has pointed out, the school-as-is performs important functions for the society. It socializes the young, helping them adapt to an impersonal and hierarchical society. It exists for the teacher as a place of employment and as a stage where he or she acts out an important life-role. For parents, it is an effective custodian, and they will approve any change that does not reduce the school's custodial effectiveness. For the young person, the school is primarily a social institution, a place to meet like-minded peers. So despite the talk of de-schooling and nonschool learning centers, the schools as we know them will continue to exist.

There is strong evidence that the schools of today are not only meeting those needs but are doing so in a way that pleases their constituents. Recent Gallup surveys attest to this fact: "The fourth annual Gallup Poll of Public Attitudes towards education indicated that only 7% of the parents felt that schools were to blame when children do poorly in school, and 66% of the parents felt that school boards were working hard to improve the quality of education" ("Fourth Annual Gallup Poll," 1972).

Yet while many schools will remain essentially as they are in their general structure, a second prevailing force is a continued concern for educational change. For years the conventional wisdom about educational change was based upon the studies of Paul Mort (1964), which held that the schools changed very little, and the pace of change was so slow that it took fifty years for any major change to be institutionalized. Recent studies, however, present us with a far different picture. The typical pattern of the past ten years, at least, has been one of rapid adoption and frequent change. The adoption of PSSC physics is a case in point: within a few years the course was adopted by most high schools in the country.

More recent evidence can be found in the proliferation of mini-courses. First introduced in a few secondary schools in the late sixties, they are now so widespread that they cease to attract attention. It seems quite likely that such faddism will continue for the next decade.

A final predictable force to be confronted is the inability of all these changes to make any real difference in the lives of the young. Too often the changes of the sort described are somewhat superficial, concerned with such structural matters as grouping strategies, staffing arrangements, and scheduling variations. And, as Christopher Jencks has pointed out, even major attempts to change the schools will not produce dramatic changes in the society: "None of the evidence we have reviewed suggests that school reform can be expected to bring about significant social changes outside the schools" (Jencks, 1972, p. 255). We will always have the poor with us—poor people and poor readers as well.

The picture, then, seems clear: the next five years—and more, probably—will see the schools functioning as they are, making frequent structural changes, and have little impact on the basic inequality of our society.

Such a picture, at first glance, will not please all of us. The radicals will throw up their hands in disgust. The reactionaries, hoping for a retreat to the past, will ridicule the changes as mindless. But the rest of us practicing meliorists, given to bargaining for small gains, should find those conclusions a source of both reassurance and challenge.

The sources of the reassurance are threefold. First, we can count on schools to exist; we need not confront radical changes that might immobilize us. Second, there will be a sanction for change that should support us even among conservative critics. Finally, as Jencks has pointed out, the limited impact of schooling on future income level frees us, in fact, from the factory model of input-output and enables us instead to think of school as a family (Jencks, 1972, p. 256).

The challenge is even more important: we have committed ourselves to educating all the youth in the established schools; it is incumbent on us to find ways of making those schools more responsive to the diverse needs of the students they serve. The reasonable person, therefore, rejects the cry of the radical that the burning question is how to destroy the school. He or she also rejects the complaint of the cynical critic that no change is possible. The only important question left is: in a time when change is sanctioned, in a context where the experience of schooling is more important than its product, what changes do we implement in the conventional school?

The author does not intend to offer one more panacea, one more instant solution to the problems these schools face. Instead, he would argue, for several reasons, that the only reasonable answer is to provide for teacher, student, and parent, a wide range of options and alternatives: alternative organizational patterns, alternative curricula, alternative teaching styles, alternative learning strategies.

The first reason for proposing alternatives is that there is abundant evidence that students differ markedly in several important dimensions. For years we have acknowledged that they differ in physical maturation, intelligence, and general school achievement. But there are even more important differences that make the quest for some single solution a futile one at best. As Harold E. and Mary Cover Jones (1962), indicate, children differ significantly in such important dimensions as cycles of growth, reactions to physical characteristics, mental growth, personality development, attitudes toward the peer culture, sexual identity, value orientations, concern for leadership and prestige, and preference for independence.

Not only do the students differ markedly, but the nature of learning is multiple, not single. Philip Phenix (1964), among others, has pointed out that the several ways of knowing are so significantly different that they constitute separate disciplines, mastered in quite different ways. Our own commonsense experience tells us, for instance, that learning to write a poem is quite different from learning to prove a theorem in geometry.

This diversity in students and in learning suggests that we shall never find the ideal teacher, method, or climate for learning. To begin with, we should know by this time that there is no ideal teacher, even though the naïve insist that the projection of their own idiosyncrasies represents some optimal combination of characteristics. Percival Symonds, who has spent more time than other educators studying teacher personality, concluded his studies with this insight:

> It is valuable to have many different types of personalities serve as teachers so that children may learn something from each—security, application, order, initiative, curiosity, co-operation, ambition, responsibility, consideration for others, etc. No one person as a teacher could contribute to each of these in equal degree. I doubt if we shall ever know enough to say that this or that personality type is most desirable to teach our children [Symonds, 1950, p. 696].

The search for some ideal method is similarly doomed to failure. After decades of study and painstaking research, we can conclude only that no single method in and of itself is superior to any other. Irving Lorge sums it up this way:

> It would be happy indeed if there were a clear answer on the relative value of the different methods studied. Unfortunately, this is not so. The experimental literature allows every teacher to find support for any method. Experimentally, the lecture method has been demonstrated to be the best, the average, and the worst method. Similar generalizations can be made for the discussion and the recitation method. . . . It is not surprising, therefore, that despite the fact that more than one hundred studies have been made of contrasting methods, the adequacy of any method is still indeterminate [Lorge, 1954, p. 167].

What of school climate? Is it likely that one type of climate or one set of organizational structures is better than any other? Here the evidence once more fails to support the superiority of any given kind of program. Years of study have failed to indicate conclusively that nongraded grouping, differentiated staffing, modular scheduling, flexible grouping, or any other organizational method accounts for significant differences in student achievement. One major work, in fact, has given strong support to the contention that school environments have differential impact on groups of students. A comprehensive study of different school environments by Patricia Minuchin and her colleagues concluded that the "traditional" school and the "modern" school had quite different effects on the children enrolled, and that the effects varied with the child. "In any of these environments some children were successful and some floundered, but not the same kinds of children in each, nor in the same way" (Minuchin et al., 1969, p. 405).

The argument, therefore, is simple and, hopefully, cogent: students vary significantly. Learning is of diverse sorts. No type of teacher, method, or climate is inherently superior. Thus a range of teachers, methods, and climates will better respond to the varied needs of students in mastering different types of learning. So the solution of the seventies is multiplicity, diversity, and choice.

One final phase of the answer needs explicating here. The author believes that such alternatives should be developed locally, offered in small autonomous units, and structured so that they are easy to implement and discard.

The first factor, local development of alternatives, is a straightforward rejection of "teacher-proof curricula" developed by some curriculum laboratory and imposed on a local staff. While several models will be presented for consideration in this work, the intent is not to presume to prescribe for a local staff, for the author is totally committed to participant control. Such a commitment is based, first of all, upon the belief that participant-developed solutions are more likely to be responsive to the special needs and interests of the students. Although adolescents have very similar needs and interests, the author feels there are enough idiosyncratic differences among student populations that the school program will be more attractive and effective if it is locally developed.

The other argument for participant control is that teachers will feel more committed to a solution they have developed. Our participation in a solution commits us emotionally to it, and we are more likely to devote unflagging energies to making it succeed. We also need to feel a greater sense of power and control over our own lives. And the ability to shape a school program will restore to the participants some sense of power and autonomy.

Why are small schools and small units needed? There is, first of all, a persuasive logic in reasoning that smaller units make it easier for people to relate more directly and more personally to each other. The large school requires bureaucratic structures for control, and the bureaucracy necessarily intrudes upon direct relationships between people. Personal relationships also seem easier to come by in a school of fifty than they do in a school of 4,000. While students will always form their own cliques and crowds regardless of the size of the school, the interpersonal complexity of large institutions makes personal relationships beyond the confines of the crowd hard to come by in the very large school.

The logical arguments in favor of smaller units are supported by some significant research on the impact of school size. For example, Ibrahim Hussein's study showed that teachers in larger schools felt less job satisfaction (Hussein, 1968). Edwin P. Willens (1967) found that the marginal student in the small school was more likely to participate in school activities than similar students in larger schools. And Urban J. Leavitt's study concluded that the optimum size interval may be between 200 and 699 students and that the best personnel usage was in the 200–399 range (Leavitt, 1960).

Small autonomous units can also respond better to rapid change than larger bureaucratic organizations. And continuing change confronts us for the foreseeable future. As Alvin Toffler (1970) and others have pointed out, rapid change seems to be endemic to this age and our society. And the schools will experience this change more sharply perhaps than any other institution. All across the country, teachers comment that "students are not the same anymore." And the chances are that they will continue to change in their attitudes toward adults, in their motivations to learn, in their short-term goals and aspirations. The curriculum will change, as new knowledge develops at an ever-accelerating rate. New technology, probably in the form of sophisticated video cassette retrieval systems and simple classroom computers, will change the role of the teacher.

The large bureaucratic organization cannot respond quickly enough to such rapid change. The largeness of the organization simply makes it less sensitive to change and complicates the information flow necessary for effective change. The hierarchical nature of the large school gives those in authority a vested interest in resisting change, and they will prefer that a cumbersome committee study problems. And experience tells us that the problems will vanish or become a crisis before a large committee can solve them.

On the other hand, the small unit typically has more open communication and is better able to sense change coming. Typically, those who lead the smaller unit have less need to control and to expand authority; they are thus more receptive to change. And the smallness of the unit enables everyone involved to deal with the problem directly and to solve it expeditiously.

The author obviously tends to agree with Warren G. Bennis' view:

> The social structure of organizations of the future will have some unique characteristics. The key word will be "temporary." There will be adaptive, rapidly changing temporary systems. These will be task forces organized around problems. . . . The group will be arranged on an organic rather than mechanical model; it will evolve in response to a problem rather than to programmed role expectations [Bennis, 1968, pp. 73–74].

The argument for simple solutions easily installed also grows out of the need for rapid change. In the past, schools have typically spent a few years studying a problem, a few years planning the solution, and a few years implementing it in a gradual process. We no longer can afford the luxury of deliberate study and long-term planning. Change comes so rapidly that we should embrace a playful faddism: smelling problems, trying a solution, adopting another new program. And only simple solutions without administrative complexity can fit such a paradigm.

Such a proposal clearly rejects the change model advocated by Ronald G. Havelock (1970), which posits a specially designated "change agent" operating systematically to implement carefully planned change over a period of time. Instead of some single "change agent" arriving from outside the organization, the entire staff should be change agents. Each teacher becomes charged with the task of identifying problems and proposing solutions. And instead of a systems approach to controlled change, an organic process should be used in which changes are proposed, examined briefly for feasibility, implemented without undue fuss, and designed to self-destruct within a few years.

All these arguments seem to add up to the conclusion that in educational planning, instead of looking for some single answer, we should be providing multiple options. At every stage of children's development, we should be offering them and their parents a variety of learning environments, curricula, and teaching styles through small autonomous units. And the installation and implementation of these options should be simple enough for them to be adopted readily and jettisoned easily, so that we never again are trapped by obsolescence.

This book is about options for the future. It does not tout any single programmatic solution. It does not sell some new package. Rather it argues for variety, diversity, multiplicity, options. It says only that alternatives are needed.

What kinds of alternatives are needed and in what types of structures should they be developed? The answers, of course, are as numerous as their advocates: we have seen during recent years an almost bewildering proliferation of alternatives. For purposes of analysis, these options will be examined systematically under the rubrics of alternative schools, alternative programs, and alternative paths. While some attempt will be made here at stipulative definitions that will distinguish these terms for most cases, in many instances the terms will overlap. In such instances we must rely upon how the staff itself perceives its own offerings, whether as school, program, or path. Given that limitation, the following definitions are offered:

1. *Alternative school:* A small school, which students may choose to attend in place of the conventional school, that is significantly different from conventional schools, and typically emphasizes a high degree of staff and student involvement in decision making. Ordinarily the alternative school occupies separate facilities. Even in those few instances where it is housed in the same building as the conventional school, it is designated here as an alternative school if it is an autonomous instructional unit, with its own territory, leadership, rules, and budget. Typically, its offerings encompass the entire range of the curriculum; in a few cases, however, an autonomous and separate school will provide for only part of the student's program. For our purposes the importance of separateness and autonomy lie in the budget, decision making, and leadership, not essentially in program and facilities.

2. *Alternative program:* A unit within a larger and more conventional school, dependent upon the parent school for budget, resources, and authority, offering a program of studies significantly different from those of the conventional school, elected voluntarily by students and their parents. The alternative program may encompass all or part of the student's educational experience; its designation as a dependent program relates to its lack of autonomy in governance, budgeting, and decision making.

3. *Alternative paths:* Some special provision and arrangement through which individual students can plan their own programs, making extensive use of resources (people, places, materials) outside the regular school setting. In a conventional school which does not provide alternative programs to groups of students, alternative paths make it possible for individual students to plan their own programs of alternative study, which typically would involve such arrangements as

apprenticeships, correspondence study, independent projects, and courses by television.

Obviously, the author does not argue that one of these alternative arrangements is better than another. Each of these approaches—alternative schools, alternative programs, alternative paths—has its own strengths and weaknesses. The intent here is to describe each of these approaches, to suggest their implications for the schools of today and tomorrow, and to provide practical suggestions about their implementation.

The book begins with an overview of alternative schools, since they provide us with a fresh orientation about what can be done and subsume in their characteristics the options available for alternative programs and paths. Then alternative programs and paths are examined as optional structures. In succeeding chapters the specific types of alternatives available in facilities, staffing, curricula, and so on are examined. And the book concludes with some practical suggestions for the next steps that schools can take.

While the central concern of this work is with secondary school students and their education, the options suggested make a great deal of sense for both elementary children and postsecondary youth. At every level of education more options are needed, more choices are essential.

The only choice the author does not sanction is the choice of not changing.

References

Bennis, Warren G. "Beyond Bureaucracy," in *The Temporary Society*, by Warren G. Bennis and Philip E. Slater. New York. Harper and Row, 1968.

Dreeben, Robert. *On What Is Learned in School*. Reading, Massachusetts: Addison-Wesley, 1968.

"Fourth Annual Gallup Poll of Public Attitudes Towards Education," *Phi Delta Kappan*, 54 (September 1972).

Havelock, Ronald G. "Planning for Innovation," Ann Arbor: Center for Research in the Utilization of Scientific Knowledge, University of Michigan, 1970.

Hussein, Ibrahim M. "The Effect of School Size upon Teacher Satisfaction and Participation." (Unpublished doctor's thesis, The University of Michigan, 1968.) Dissertation Abstracts: 29: 2480-A, 1969.

Illich, Ivan D. *Deschooling Society*. New York: Harper and Row, 1971.

Jencks, Christopher. *Inequality*. New York: Basic Books, 1972.

Jones, Harold E., and Mary Cover Jones, "Individual Differences in Early Adolescence," in *Individualizing Instruction, Sixty-First Yearbook of the National Society for the Study of Education*, Part 1, edited by Nelson B. Henry. Chicago: University of Chicago Press, 1962.

Leavitt, Urban J. "Elementary School Size Relationships." (Unpublished doctor's thesis, The University of Texas, 1960.) Dissertation Abstracts, 20: 4572, 1960.

Lorge, Irving. "If They Know Not, Teach," *Teachers College Record*, 56 (December 1954).

Minuchin, Patricia, Edna Shapiro, and Herbert Zimiles. *Psychological Impact of School Experience*. New York: Basic Books, 1969.

Mort, Paul R. "Studies in Educational Innovation from the Institute of Administrative Research," in *Innovation in Education*, edited by Matthew B. Miles. New York: Bureau of Publications, Teachers College, Columbia University, 1964.

Phenix, Philip H. *Realms of Meaning: A Philosophy of the Curriculum*. New York: McGraw-Hill, 1964.

Reich, Charles A. *The Greening of America*. New York: Random House, 1970.

Symonds, Percival. "Reflections on Observations of Teachers," *Journal of Educational Research*, 43 (May 1950), pp. 688–696.

Toffler, Alvin. *Future Shock*. New York: Random House, 1970.

Willens, Edwin P. "Sense of Obligation to High School Activities as Related to School Size and Marginality of Student," *Child Development*, Vol. 38, No. 4 (December 1967), pp. 1247–1260.

Chapter Two

Alternative Schools: The Basic Framework

It has been argued thus far that, while the conventional public and parochial schools will probably continue to provide a basic education for most youth, more options and choices are needed in the form of alternative schools, alternative programs, and alternative paths. This chapter examines the options of the autonomous alternative school, offered within the existing systems. The chapter reviews the arguments for and against such separate schools within the system, provides a schema for planning and describing such schools, and concludes with an identification of the most common types.

Why Alternatives Within the System?

The alternative school movement seems to be growing. And it should grow even more—public and parochial school systems should open up additional alternative schools. The objective in this section, therefore, is to present a reasoned defense for the further development of alternative schools.

The author does not intend, however, to fall into the trap of arguing that alternative schools are "better than" conventional schools. Only a fool or an ideologue would attempt such a risky and fruitless venture.

Such a venture is hazardous on at least three counts. One is the obvious diversity of both alternative and conventional schools: there are some exciting alternative schools and some boring ones, and there are some exciting conventional schools and some boring ones.

The second difficulty is that no one really agrees what "better" means in operational terms. We can all subscribe to a lofty goal, such as "the schools will develop in the young person a sense of personal autonomy." When we try to put that goal into operation, however, we begin to fight: is a black boy who attacks a racist teacher showing personal autonomy or disturbing the peace?

Even when we agree that all schools should develop basic learning competencies, we face the third difficulty: our existing measures for assessing short-term growth are not good enough to provide valid data. As a consequence, those few evaluative studies which have attempted comparisons almost always conclude with the frustrating "no significant difference." For example, Nicolaus Mills' review of the research on free and directed schools concluded in this way:

> The only conclusion supported by this survey is one that reinforces previous evidence on the question of free versus directed schools: in terms of conventional tests and cognitive skills, students educated in directed schools tend to do slightly better than those educated in free schools, but the difference is slight and in no way supports a claim for the overall superiority of one or the other kind of school [Mills, 1971, p. 9].

The author, therefore, will not attempt to prove that alternative schools are "better." Instead, he will reason logically from a few basic assumptions, some honest preferences, and some very limited evidence that it makes good sense to open alternative schools, as a complement to existing schools.

To begin with, however, fairness leads us to review the arguments against alternatives.

The first set of arguments comes from supposedly "objective" sociologists. One argument, persuasively stated by Robert Dreeben (1968) and others, is that the conventional school is needed to socialize youth and help them accept the norms of competitive and bureaucratic institutions. One response is to remind ourselves that there is plenty of that all around us: the community, the church, the factory, the Little League are all doing their share in developing enterprising capitalists. The other response emerges from the personal bias of the liberal, who sees a society suffering from excessive bureaucratization and competition and wants to make some changes now.

A second sociological argument against alternatives is that they result in racial or social class stratification and are not as effective as the comprehensive school in serving as a melting pot. There is some merit to this charge, and educational planners need to weigh the gains and losses of such stratification. There are, however, three ways of rebutting this argument. One is to realize that the so-called comprehensive high school will always exist for those who want to be melted. The second is to point out, as C.B. Nam and J.D. Cowhig (1962) have shown, that extensive stratification is often imposed by the so-called comprehensive school through its ability-grouping devices. And the third is to conclude that self-imposed stratification is more defensible in a democracy than the institutionally imposed brand.

The second group of critics includes those of the educational right, who attack the legitimacy of alternative schools, pointing out the mindlessness of the curriculum, the messiness of the place, and the anarchy of the school society. Once we discount the rhetorical excesses of such claims, we can admit that some alternative schools stress too much occult nonsense (like some of their conventional counterparts), many are messy places (similar to the cafeteria of your neighborhood high school), and some spend too much time arguing about decisions on how to make decisions (unlike the high school on the hill). But the most persuasive answer is that no idea should be attacked because of the excesses of its most foolish advocates. The basic notion of an alternative school is that the school will be able to develop just as much or as little academic rigor, lavatory cleanliness, and leader autocracy as its participants desire. This seems to be one of the basic notions of a democracy.

The third group of critics includes those on the radical left, who are so thoroughly disenchanted with the system that reformism is more damned than conservatism. The most articulate of these is certainly Allen Graubard, who expresses his views in this fashion: "My firm view is that attempts at truly humanizing the public schools must run up against the fundamental social realities—the sickness of American society. The liberal dream of cure by means of education is misconceived. As I mentioned before, this realization is most directly relevant to public school reformers" (Graubard, 1972, p. 260).

The only rational answer to this argument is to say that the author differs both in how he sees that society and where he stands as a consequence of his perspective. His view is that the American society is like a healthy man with a serious case of the flu, not like an invalid with a terminal case of cancer. The consequence is that he stands inside the system, reforming, not revolutionizing.

Obviously, opening up public school alternatives will not please conventional sociologists, hidebound academics, or radical critics. How will such alternatives appeal to the schoolteacher, administrator, and student? What reasonable arguments can be advanced in favor of alternative schools to those presently working within the system?

The first response is to put the matter in perspective. The small alternative school is designed to supplement, not replace, the existing school. Those who prefer bigness, adult control, student councils, and football teams can stay where they are and enjoy the benefits accruing thereto.

The second response concerns economic feasibility. Alternative schools can be operated at the same or for a lower per pupil cost than can the conventional school. As Mario D. Fantini (1973) has pointed out, the use of noncertificated teachers, the utilization of existing space, and the ability to teach without expensive hardware makes the alternative school a real bargain.

The third response emerges from a value system which sees diversity and choice as desirable ends unto themselves. Students, teachers, and learning differ; therefore, diversity of environment, structure, and curriculum is good. But diversity without choice is meaningless. If students were to be assigned to these diverse schools by some educator playing god, then we would risk returning to a closed society where decisions are made by those who think they know better.

The final argument is based more upon intuition than hard data. In an age of alienation, the most critical task for educators is to create learning communities where each person feels known, is valued, and receives respect. These fuzzy, imprecise goals may be more attainable in a small alternative school than they are in a large bureaucratic institution. If people have a chance to dream their own visions, to shape their own reality, the world seems just a little bit better.

What Kinds of Alternatives?

If it seems desirable, then, to develop alternative schools, the question becomes one of determining the kinds of alternatives which can be offered. In this section alternative schools are classified for purposes of analysis and planning.

One useful way of classifying alternatives has been proposed by Ralph Hansen (n.d., p. 6). Beset by almost a bewildering array of alternatives, he developed a three-dimensional cell to enable us to sort out types and categories of alternatives. His model is shown in Figure 1. Clearly, such an approach indicates the diversity possible among alternative schools; it yields forty-eight alternative types.

Yet even such a three-dimensional analysis does not sufficiently cover all the permutations available to the educator planning or describing an alternative program. It is useful in both the planning and the describing tasks to use a more complex classification schema, which focuses systematically on the twenty most significant characteristics of alternative schools and indicates three typical options to planners and analysts. Figure 1 presents such a schema. The following discussion comments on and explains some of the more important features.

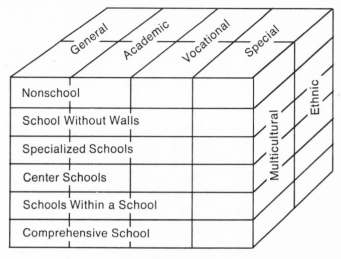

Figure 1

Note first the organization of this schema. It has been structured so that it can be used as a guideline for planning, with the characteristics listed and described in an order that represents an optimal planning sequence. Later the business of planning for options will be discussed in greater detail; this section simply presents an overview of the planning sequence.

The Source of the School—Funds and Control

Questions 1 and 2 deal with the basic sources of the school—its origins and its fiscal resources.

1. What is the source of funding? An increasing number of alternative schools, like most of those in Philadelphia, Pennsylvania, are supported entirely with local tax dollars; such funding probably provides for the greatest amount of security and ensures the maximum local commitment. Many schools, at least in the first few years of their existence, draw upon state and federal funds or special grants from private foundations; in the early seventies, for example, the Office of Experimental Schools of the Office of Education funded several alternative schools in Berkeley, California. While such federal grants ease

the financial burdens during the first critical years, they involve a high degree of risk, since federal funds are subject to the whims of Congress and the caprices of the president. Most of the small free schools and freedom schools are supported entirely by tuition and contributions; in fact, many of the leaders of the free school movement feel that any other kind of funding is either immoral or unduly restrictive. Such funding permits the maximum ideological freedom; but it is equally precarious, and many free school directors seem to spend an inordinate amount of time raising and collecting money.

2. Where is the ultimate source of control? An increasing number of alternative schools are part of the public school system, responsible to a district school board. A small handful of alternative schools are church-related, most of them private schools that once prided themselves on being academically elite and have now moved toward an alternative educational style. And a large number of alternative schools are truly independent, responsible only to their board of directors or some faculty-parent group.

The Nature of the Student Body

3. Who are the students that the school serves? In many ways, this is the central question from which everything else follows. In any planning sequence this question perhaps should be one of the first raised; once the target population and its needs have been identified, all matters of governance and program can be decided better. Alternative schools have developed an interesting variety of answers. On the one hand, some explicitly try to get a heterogeneous student body, even though they realize a certain kind of homogeneity results from self-selection. On the other hand, some alternative schools recruit only certain types of students—dropouts, drug users, disruptive students, artistically talented, or some other special group. While the heterogeneous student body is probably more interesting and challenging, a sense of community is probably easier to develop when the students have in common something more than the desire to attend that school.

Boundaries and Power

With the student body tentatively identified, the next group of decisions deals with the critical tasks of power delineation and boundary setting.

4. How active is the policy-making board? Some alternative schools are really operated by their staffs, with the official board functioning primarily as window dressing. At the other extreme, some of the freedom schools with close community ties are in reality controlled by the citizen board, which takes an active interest in the day-to-day affairs of the school.

5. Who is primarily responsible for the day-to-day governance of the school? In most alternative schools, despite their rhetoric of participatory decision making, the teachers are clearly in charge, with the students being only nominally involved. In a few of the more radical alternative schools, the students seem really to be in charge; since they outnumber the faculty, they have the deciding vote when pure democracy is practiced. In a few schools there is a sincere attempt to stake out areas for staff decision making, areas for student decision making, and areas of shared influence.

6. What is the nature of the on-site leadership? This question has provoked violent controversy within the movement. On the one hand, there are those like Jonathan Kozol (1972) who argue that a single strong leader is needed, often a charismatic figure who pulls the school through a continuing series of crises. On the other hand, some very small free schools, sometimes associated with communes, practice a kind of anarchic leadership, where decisions are made by consensus or not at all. Most alternative schools are somewhere in the middle, with a strong leader working hard to get staff and student input into all critical decisions.

Location in Space and Time

The next sequence of questions examines organizational, spatial, and temporal relationships, as another level of boundary setting.

7. What is the school's relationship with the conventional schools? A small number of alternatives—like the Cambridge Free School in Massachusetts—are actually housed within the regular school and draw heavily upon the support services (cafeteria, health services, and so on) provided by the regular school. While such an arrangement is often most feasible economically and enables the staff to devote its energies to other more central problems, the arrangement also has severe drawbacks. Problems of territoriality develop with the regular school, and the alternative students often find themselves subject to two quite different sets of rules and codes of behavior. Most alternative schools have opted for complete independence, operating totally autonomous and physically separate units. The trade-off is obvious. They gain more freedom but have more problems with facilities and services. Several alternative schools have tried to have the best of both worlds by operating as a semidetached annex to the regular school; the School for Human Services, for example, is an annex of the John Bartram High School in Philadelphia. Such annexes typically keep their students on the attendance rolls of the conventional school and recommend that the regular school issue a diploma when its staff feels that the alternative school student has qualified for it. Such annex arrangements have unique advantages; the main drawback is that, being neither fish nor fowl, the school spends much time negotiating questions of final authority.

8. What type of facilities should be used? Many alternative schools are housed in old school buildings that the district abandoned in favor of new ones; such old buildings constructed in the early decades of this century are still in sound condition and seem to make suitable environments for alternative schools. Some schools, like the early Parkway Program, have no single building but use the varied resources of the city; in such cases a warehouse loft often doubles as offices and assembly room, with the students leaving this home base for learning throughout the city. And many alternative schools are housed in very unconventional facilities, such as abandoned factories, empty dormitories, and vacated supermarkets.

9. Is the alternative school viewed as all or part of the student's education? In a few cases the alternative school is seen as only a part of the student's secondary education—either as a part of each year or as one full year in a three-year program. The Freedom School in Washington, D.C., for example, provides a black-oriented curriculum for part of the student's day; in the other half of the day he or she attends the regular school, taking conventional courses. The Pennsylvania Advancement School in Philadelphia previously enrolled junior high school students for a year, after which they returned to their regular school. While such "part-time" schools are often attacked as being "fragmented," they do seem to offer an attractive alternative for the student who is not ready for a full commitment to the alternative school. Most alternative schools, however, ask for and get a full commitment from the student—he or she spends a whole day there and is expected to attend until graduation. In passing, this observation might be offered: as the number and variety of alternative schools grow, it seems quite likely that in a typical four-year high school sequence a student might spend one year at each of three quite different alternatives and one year at the regular school.

Teaching and Staffing

The next phase of planning probably should include determinations about the composition and relationships of the staff.

10. What type of staff should be used? A few alternative schools use only fully certificated teachers, perhaps because they are bound by state or local restrictions or because they were started by a small group of certificated teachers who do not see a need to bring in others. On the other hand, some of the radical free schools pride themselves on not using certificated teachers at all, relying almost entirely on parents and other concerned adults to provide the instructional expertise. Most of the alternative schools seem to be somewhere in the middle, using a small core staff of certificated teachers supplemented with a variety of noncertificated volunteers and part-time paid help.

11. How should the staff be organized? A few alternative schools use a differentiated staffing pattern, with two or three levels of leadership and many specialized functions (director, head teacher, team leader, reading specialist, etc.). Most alternative schools, however, reject such a practice as being too bureaucratic and undemocratic; they work hard to maintain a flat table of organization, one in which there are no specialists and no differences in status. In the latter form, for example, every teacher is considered a reading teacher and is expected to act as a guidance counselor.

Student Selection, Retention, and Program Evaluation

With the staff selected or at least the process identified, the planning can next move to decisions about student selection, student retention, and program evaluation, the final group of decisions which can rightfully be made without student and parent input.

12. How will students be selected? In a handful of the alternative schools (usually those for the disruptive), students are assigned to the school, with only a minimal amount of choice; in most of the free schools, anyone who walks in off the street is welcomed. Most of the alternative schools connected with the public school system permit all interested students to apply, selecting by lottery those to be admitted. While critics of the lottery system argue that many of the students who "most need" the alternative school are excluded by the luck of the draw, the defenders retort that it is the only fair system—since no one can determine in advance who "most needs" the alternative school.

13. Will students ever be required to leave the school? Since the conventional schools have often been criticized for excluding students who don't fit in, most alternative schools are reluctant to follow the same practice. However, since they usually do not punish with detention or suspension, some schools find that the only sanction they have for controlling behavior is exclusion; they therefore set up rules and procedures by which students may be requested to leave the school.

The free schools typically make a point of not asking anyone to leave; always there is the hope that salvation is possible.

14. How should the program be evaluated? A few schools, chiefly those with federal or foundation funding, develop and carry out elaborate evaluation systems, with explicitly stated objectives and measures for determining whether those objectives have been achieved. Most free schools claim they are too busy for such formal evaluation and that their programs are working toward goals that cannot be evaluated.

Program Substance and Implementation

The final stage of the planning process includes all those substantive matters that are perhaps best determined with student and parent input.

15. How structured should the school be? "Structure" in this sense focuses on the question of how much adult control and direction are desired. A few of the freedom schools developed by and for blacks and other ethnic minorities are openly proud of the fact that they operate a "tight ship"; their leaders contend that young people from those ethnic groups seem to thrive best in a highly ordered world with strong adult authority. On the other hand, many of the free schools espouse a child-centered permissiveness, arguing that only as the child experiences total freedom can he or she learn to be free. Most alternative schools seem to be struggling along a middle path, having students and staff together develop a few simple rules that all agree to accept. Those in this middle group argue quite strongly, in fact, that this "boundary setting" is one of the most important functions the school should accomplish before it opens for the first day.

16. What is the general nature of the school's program? A few alternative schools offer rather conventional programs in unconventional environments. Here again the freedom schools serving black communities argue that their students need basic skills and solid subjects, not the "basket-weaving" curriculum of the free schools. But the free schools argue that their curriculum is rightly built around students' interests and the

staff's competencies; their programs consequently feature such unconventional offerings as "stained glass making," "the Marxism of Mao," "how to survive in the city without spending money," and "the politics of hunger." Most of the alternative schools seem to find themselves in the middle, often pushed there by the demands of parents or the anxieties of students, offering standard courses in science, mathematics, and foreign languages, supplemented with a healthy mixture of the esoteric.

17. How should students be grouped for instruction? This question, which often absorbs the attention of conventional school administrators, does not loom very large in the alternative school literature. Observation and correspondence indicate that in a few schools students are grouped by grade level. Most of the free schools make a point of mixing older students and very young children in some type of "family setting." Most of the public alternative schools operate nongraded programs in which students sort themselves out by interest, with such groups usually covering a three-year grade span.

18. What kind of schedule should be used? The prevailing pattern in alternative schools seems to be some type of college schedule, where students are given a list of courses, teachers, and hours and are expected to build their own schedules. Some of these fall into rather regular patterns of Monday, Wednesday, Friday, 9–10; Tuesday, Thursday, 10–11:30. Other schedules include interesting variations, with team-taught courses offered in large blocks of time, or a single day set aside for "free-form learning." At the other extreme, some of the small free schools make a point of having no schedule at all; people meet together rather spontaneously without much prearranging to exchange ideas and skills.

19. How should the pupils' progress be evaluated? Most of the alternative schools have moved away from letter grades (A, B, C, D, F). A few of the "straighter" alternative schools offer students the choice of having letter grades if they want them for college admissions, but the greater majority are using personal conferences, written evaluations, and student port-

folios, a more valid reflection of how the student is progressing. Some of the radical free schools have rejected the whole notion of evaluation and refuse to be judgmental about student progress and achievement.

20. How should schoolwork be credited? A few alternative schools use the conventional Carnegie unit as the basis for evaluating credits earned and determining eligibility for graduation. The more experimental schools use the Carnegie unit only as a general guideline and develop more flexible crediting systems. The free schools tend to reject the whole notion of credits and simply let the student determine when he or she is ready to graduate.

These twenty questions should both assist in the planning process and be useful in describing the significant features of a given school.

Some Types to Consider

Both the Hansen model and the author's own analytical schema would suggest that alternative schools could be categorized into at least forty-eight separate classes. While such systematic categorization might be useful to the planner or researcher, it perhaps is too complicated for the practitioner who needs less complexity. This chapter concludes, therefore, with a brief listing of the most common types of alternative schools now in existence. While there will be some overlapping in the categories, the following types should be helpful to someone planning an alternative school.

Student-Centered Alternatives

Although all alternative schools would argue that they are student-centered, this term is used here to describe several kinds of alternative schools that are identified primarily in terms of the kinds of students they serve.

1. Schools for students out of school. Many alternatives have been developed for pregnant girls and for students who

Table 1 A Taxonomy for Alternatives

Factors	Option 1	Option 2	Option 3
1. Funding	Public tax funds	Federal, state, foundations	Tuition and contributions
2. Control	Public school system	Church, university, or other institution	Parents, community
3. Students	Heterogeneous	Basically homogeneous by virtue of interest	Intentionally homogeneous on basis of predetermined criteria
4. Board	Inactive board	Moderately active board	Dominating board
5. Daily governance	Teachers	Teachers and students	Students
6. Leadership	Single strong leader	Single democratic leader or team of leaders	No single leader, decision by consensus
7. Relationships with conventional school	Housed in same building	Annex	Completely separate
8. Facilities	School building	Nonschool facility	No single building
9. Full-time or part-time program	Part of day or part of year	Chiefly full-time, with some movement back to main school	All education in alternative
10. Staff	Certificated	Chiefly certificated, with some noncertificated	Noncertificated
11. Staff organization	Differentiated	Some differentiation	No differentiation or specialization
12. Student selection	"Forced" assignment	Lottery from among applicants	Open admissions

13. Exclusion	Pupils excluded if they break rules	Only a few pupils excluded for very serious infractions	No one ever asked to leave
14. Program evaluation	Comprehensive	Minimal	None
15. Degree of structure	Highly structured and controlled	Students and staff develop minimal structure	Openly permissive
16. Nature of program	Conventional school offerings	Mixture of conventional and esoteric	Chiefly esoteric offerings
17. Grade organization	Graded	Nongraded within limits	Wide range of ages intentionally mixed
18. Schedule	College schedule	College schedule with variations	No schedule
19. Pupil grading	Letter grades with options	Noncompetitive evaluation	No evaluation at all
20. Crediting	Carnegie unit	Carnegie unit with variations	No credit

have dropped out or have been pushed out of school. Several of these operate in the late afternoon and evening, since these students are often working. Number Nine, in New Haven, Connecticut, was one of the first of such schools.

2. Schools for disruptive students. Many of Philadelphia's alternative schools were explicitly designed to provide a better environment for disruptive adolescents who could not adjust to the large school.

3. Schools for special ethnic groups. Several of Berkeley's alternative schools were developed specifically for black, Spanish-speaking, or some other clearly identified ethnic group.

4. Schools for the gifted and talented. Some schools are developed explicitly for the gifted. In a sense, the elite academic schools found in the big cities (such as Boston Latin and Central High School in Philadelphia) could be considered early alternatives; Murray Road in Newton, Massachusetts, is a more recent example.

Program-Centered Alternatives

All alternative schools, of course, develop their own programmatic emphases. There are, however, four kinds of alternatives that seem to be primarily program-centered.

1. Career schools. The career education movement of the seventies has led to the development of some career alternatives. The Career Academy, operated by Research for Better Schools, and the Urban Career Education Center, operated by Opportunities Industrialization Corporation, are both public career alternatives in Philadelphia.

2. Performing arts schools. Several of the big cities have long had special schools for the performing arts, where the chief emphasis is on an arts-centered curriculum. The New York High School for the Performing Arts is one of the oldest and best known.

3. Skills-training schools. Some alternative schools begin with an explicit commitment to a "hard" curriculum centering on the basic learning skills. Several of the Berkeley experimental schools were conceived with this emphasis.

4. Open learning schools. Perhaps most of the alternative schools now developing begin with a primary commitment to some vaguely defined "open curriculum," often stressing community-based learning. The St. Paul Open School in Minnesota is one of the oldest and reportedly most successful.

Place-Centered Alternatives

The final class of alternatives take their primary identity from the place where they are located or the area they serve. Here again, we can identify four common types.

1. Schools without walls. Several of the larger cities now have alternatives that are chiefly identified by the fact that they use the whole city as their classroom. Parkway in Philadelphia was the first.

2. Community schools. Several small alternative schools began with a close identification with their community. Most such schools are located in black neighborhoods and have a strong measure of local control, even when they are part of the system. The West Philadelphia Free School is one of many such schools.

3. Multi-district schools. Some alternative schools come into being when several school districts decide to work together. The Alternative Schools Project in suburban Philadelphia, Pennsylvania, serves six different school districts.

4. Wilderness schools. Outward Bound is one of a few alternative programs that offer an education by forcing the participants to confront the natural environment.

So the educator working inside the system has a choice when deciding about a type of alternative school: he or she can begin with Hansen's forty-eight combinations, the author's own schema, the twelve common types—or throw away the typology and begin to dream. The important thing is to begin.

How do you begin? A general sequence has been suggested in the schema above. At this juncture the author would like to suggest a calendar for planning, realizing full well that each district and school system will have its own approach. The author prefers a short period of planning with clear delineation of shared responsibility.

As the calendar which is outlined in Table 2 indicates, the impetus for the school can come from several sources—students, teachers, parents, or school administrators. There is no single place where change begins. For example, the original idea for the Alternative Schools Project in Elkins Park, Pennsylvania, came from the superintendents of suburban school districts near Philadelphia.

No more than eight months' lead time is required for the entire planning process. The critical planning takes place once students and staff have been selected, not much before.

Following the surfacing of the original idea for the alternative school, the chief school administrator gets board approval, determines the amount and source of funds, and agrees with the board about the source of control of the school. Following the setting of these broad limits, the board and administrator should appoint a representative planning task force, which would carry out the important early planning until the staff and students themselves could take over the planning. Obviously, the task force should include administrators, teachers, parents, students, and the wider community.

The planning task force, under the leadership of an acting chairman, identifies the general student population to be served and conducts an assessment of the target population's needs. The data from this needs assessment will be useful in later stages of the planning process and in making the next sequence of decisions. There are two basic approaches to this stage of the planning process. One approach is to decide in advance to open a certain kind of alternative school—such as a school without walls—find out who applies and is selected, and then assess the needs of the students actually chosen for the school, using the data from the assessment for later stages of the planning. The second approach is perhaps more rational and logical. It begins by identifying the target population to be served—for example, unmotivated students from disadvantaged backgrounds. Planners then proceed by finding a student population similar to the target population, and using the data to begin the planning process.After the planning process is well under way, the actual students are selected, and the data are modified, if necessary, to accommodate those actually enrolling. Either process can work effectively; the important matter is to get reliable data as soon as possible about the nature and needs of the population to be served.

Based on that data, the task force then recommends to the board and chief administrator some general policies concerning governance and policy making, proposing some guidelines for the selection of the leader and the nature of the leader's role. With the approval of the board and the chief administrator, these guidelines are used to facilitate the selection of the leader or director. Acting within the broad policy guidelines established by the board, the director and task force make decisions about the location of the school and the extent of the program.

The staff members are then selected, with the nature of the staff significantly influenced by the data derived from the needs assessment. At this stage the staff and director assume control of the planning process, and the planning task force is dissolved. The staff and director decide about the nature of staff organization and the process of student selection. With these selection guidelines established, the students are chosen.

With the assistance of the staff, the director sets up several staff-student-parent action task forces to make recommendations concerning the day-to-day operation of the school and to make a final determination concerning the crucial matter of rules governing student behavior. These decisions then become guidelines for the day-to-day operation of the school, but are modified as necessary once the school opens and the ideals of the planning stage are tested in the setting of the real school.

Finally, two months after school begins, the director, staff, and students meet in intensive problem-solving sessions. Now they know the reality and have identified the actual problems. So they close school and take stock.

This planning model has certain features which make it a significant departure from other models and commend it especially to alternative school planners. First, there is the shortness of this particular planning cycle. The author does not be-

Table 2 Planning Calendar for Alternative Schools

Primary Thrust	Date	Task	Primarily Responsible
Boundary setting	December	Impetus for school develops.	Students, parents, teachers, or administrators
	January	System board approval secured.	Chief school administrator
		Decision made about funding and control.	Board, chief administrator
		Task force appointed.	Board, chief administrator
Policy making	February	Student population identified, needs assessment made.	Planning task force
		Decisions made concerning leadership and policy making.	Planning task force recommends to board.
		Director selected.	Planning task force recommends to board.
Constituency forming	March	Decisions made about location of school and extent of program.	Director with planning task force
	April	Staff selected.	Director and planning task force
		Decisions made concerning staff organization and student selection process.	Director and staff
		Students selected.	Director, using guidelines developed

Decision making	May	Action task forces appointed.	Director and staff
	May-July	Action task forces study and make recommendations concerning day-to-day operation.	Action task forces recommend.
	September	School opens.	Director, staff, students
Problem solving	November	School closes for one week for intensive problem solving.	Director, staff, students

lieve in extended planning, since extended planning leads to overplanning for other people. Those involved in the school should assume control over the shape and form of the school, insofar as this is possible.

Second, the primary planning agent shifts as the planning progresses. In the initial stage, which has been termed "boundary setting," the funding board and its chief administrator are responsible; their concern is to establish the broad boundaries within which the school will operate.

During the next stage, policy making, a planning task force takes over. As indicated before, this task force immediately involves representatives of the groups to be served. The task force will be a small group, charged solely with the responsibility of developing recommendations for policies so that the planning can continue to move while a director is being chosen.

In the succeeding stage the director becomes primarily responsible, using the planning task force as an advisory group. The chief task during this stage is "constituency forming," or selecting staff and students. Once the staff and students have been selected, they take over, working with the director in action task forces to make the real decisions that will affect the day-to-day operation of the school.

The third feature, which relates to this agency shift, is the nature of the planning changes. In the early stages the concerns are broad and general; in later stages, immediate and specific. A decision about funding is made far in advance by a somewhat remote and official board; a decision about the school schedule is made shortly before school begins by the staff and students who will be directly affected.

Finally, the model includes specific time for a problem-solving session two months after school has opened. Now the staff and students know about problems which could not even have been predicted in August, and they can start to solve them with a new sense of urgency.

Other planning models, of course, can be developed. The important concerns are to plan intensively over a short period of time, to avoid overplanning for other people, and to move the locus of control as quickly as possible to those who will have to make the school work.

References

Dreeben, Robert. *On What Is Learned in School*. Reading, Massachusetts: Addison-Wesley, 1968.

Fantini, Mario D. *Public Schools of Choice*. New York: Simon and Schuster, 1973.

Graubard, Allen. *Free the Children*. New York: Random House, 1972.

Hansen, Ralph K. "Are Optional Alternative Public Schools Viable?" *Changing Schools*, (n.d.).

Kozol, Jonathan. *Free Schools*. Boston: Houghton Mifflin, 1972.

Mills, Nicolaus. "Free Versus Directed Schools: Benefits for the Disadvantaged?" *IRCD Bulletin*, Vol. 7, No. 4 (September 1971).

Nam, C. B., and J. D. Cowhig. "Factors Related to College Attendance of Farm and Nonfarm High School Graduates." Washington, D.C.: Government Printing Office, 1962.

CHAPTER THREE

Alternative
Programs
The separate and autonomous alternative
school is one way to provide choices in education. A second
type of option is the alternative program, defined as an educational program which is part of an existing school, significantly
different from the mainstream program, and chosen by the students enrolled. This chapter examines briefly the history of
such programs, discusses their advantages and disadvantages
as compared with alternative schools, considers the types of
alternative programs currently being offered, and concludes
with some recommendations.

History of Alternative Programs

In order to examine the background of the alternative program concept, we probably should look at its major components: (1) a smaller administrative unit within the larger
school, (2) a program significantly different from the mainstream program and (3) a program freely chosen by the students in that school.

The idea that large schools should subdivide into smaller
units has a long history, of course. Quite likely, the independent schools, which have long had smaller units called
"houses," borrowed the idea from the influential Ivy League

colleges. Thus, when public schools in the decade of the fifties began looking for ways to mitigate the effects of bigness, they had a model ready at hand. As a consequence, some new secondary schools built in the late fifties and early sixties were designed specifically to accommodate smaller units. The Hillsdale High School in San Mateo, California, and the RHAM Regional High School in Hebron, Connecticut, both opened in the late fifties, were flexibly designed to facilitate such arrangements. Yet the idea was not widely adopted, probably because of its administrative complexity. Even when the "school within a school" or "house" plan was adopted, it was used primarily as an administrative unit and had little impact on instruction. And when there was an instructional or guidance component, there was no attempt to differentiate offerings. Thus, a middle school might be structured into three houses; but students would be assigned to the house, and the three houses would have common programs.

Program differentiation has, of course, had a long history. From the earliest days of the high school, schools offered separate programs or tracks—classical, college preparatory, business, general, vocational, special. In fact, critics like Edgar Z. Friedenberg (1971) have often complained that such tracking and program differentiation schemes served only to reinforce social stratification and penalize minority groups. As such critics viewed program differentiation, they saw it only as a means of channelling the middle class into college and the lower class into the work force. Invariably, the teachers assigned to and the curricula developed for the noncollege programs were inferior to those for the college preparatory curriculum. So program differentiation is counterproductive when it becomes a device for channelling and segregating. Such effects were noted by Circuit Judge James Skelly Wright in his decision on the Hobson case. In this case, which ended the tracking system in Washington, D.C., Wright had this to say about tracking:

> Even in concept the track system is undemocratic and discriminatory. Its creator admits that it is designed to prepare some

children for white-collar, and other children for blue-collar jobs. Considering the tests used to determine which children should receive the blue-collar special and which the white, the danger of children completing their education wearing the wrong collar is far too great for this democracy to tolerate. [*Hobson v. Hansen*, 269 F. Supp. 401, D.C. D.C. 1967].

Choice has never been an important element in the American brand of compulsory schooling. In fact, the typical pattern was one of compulsion and assignment: self-designated educational experts made all the decisions for the child and parent. When the child would begin school, what teacher would be assigned, whether the child would be promoted or retained, what kind of program he or she would be enrolled in, and when education would terminate—all such matters were considered within the purview of the educational administrator. Even at the high school level, most of the curriculum was determined by the experts. Each student studied English, social studies, mathematics, and science. The major decisions made by the adolescent were whether he would take art or music, driver training or typing.

The elective programs developed early in the seventies began to provide a limited kind of choice. Typically, in such programs a student is required to take an English credit, but he or she chooses the specific mini-courses which will constitute that elective credit. In some schools the school openly specifies which teachers will teach each course, so that the student in effect chooses a teacher as well as a course. Even when the student is able to select a teacher by choosing a course, the overall element of choice is still limited. Such elective offerings are restricted usually to disciplines of English and social studies, so that the net effect is still a great degree of compulsion and necessity in educational matters.

The concept, then, of developing smaller units, with program differentiation, available by choice, is not entirely a new idea, since its pieces have been around for some time. But as a comprehensive way of reorganizing the secondary school, with a strong emphasis upon diversity and choice, it is an idea whose time seems to have come. A survey conducted by the

National Consortium for Options in Public Education, for example, indicated that 22 percent of all alternatives could be classified as alternative programs ("Directory of Alternative Public Schools," p. 6).

The idea's timeliness should be apparent from what has been said about smallness, diversity, and choice. As the alternative program idea is compared with the single monolithic school, it is strongly apparent that the smallness of the program, the differentness of its program and its climate, and the element of choice make the alternative program more attractive than the undifferentiated school to student, parent, and educator.

Alternative Programs Versus Alternative Schools

How does the alternative program, housed as part of and dependent upon a larger unit, compare with the alternative school, with its own separate identity?

First, the alternative program has several advantages. From the administrator's point of view, it is probably less expensive to operate, since resources can be shared very simply, without adding extra expense. If the alternative program uses school staff and facilities, it may be viewed as less of an adversary by people in the system, who are often suspicious of separate "free schools." The alternative program is easier to install and to terminate, thus representing less of a commitment. It has less visibility and is thus less likely to draw parent and public criticism. From the teacher's point of view, the alternative program might seem more attractive on two grounds. There is easier access to resources: a well-equipped science laboratory is always available, and the student cafeteria is conveniently nearby. Also, it is less likely to remove the teacher from the mainstream of professional dialogue: colleagues are always available for professional, political, and personal talk. And this sense of being part of the action of the big school probably makes the alternative program seem attractive to the student as well. There is still a sense of being a part of the large school, with its swirling crowds, its big activities, and its teen-age noise and commotion.

Yet there are obvious drawbacks, as well, most of which derive from ambiguous organizational relationships. From the administrator's point of view, there are recurring difficulties involving authority, communication, and power between the alternative program and the "mother school." The teachers involved in the alternative program are never entirely sure about the scope of their policy authority and their degree of curricular autonomy. And students enrolled in the alternative program never feel a clear sense of identity or understand the nature of their accountability.

Ralph Hansen, who spent a year visiting alternative schools and programs, made this observation about the ones he had seen:

> Often they [the alternative programs] are threatening because those who staff and attend the alternative are not hesitant about expressing their beliefs. But more often than not the threat is more pervasive. By deliberate design students are afforded greater personal freedom. They move about without hall passes during class periods of the traditional school. They often dress differently. They are on a first-name basis with their teachers. This kind of threat involved the Cambridge Pilot School in a major confrontation with the school board. While not all schools within schools are overtly threatening . . . many view them as a potentential threat [Hansen, n.d., p. 9].

There seems, then, that there is no clear-cut advantage to either the alternative program or the alternative school and that the choice is best made solely on the basis of local factors. If the choice is for alternative programs, a decision must be made about organizational patterns.

Types of Alternative Programs

Alternative programs typically take one of two basic organizational forms, when viewed from the perspective of the larger school unit: the limited alternative and the comprehensive. The term "limited alternative program" is used here to describe the common situation in which one large school offers one or two alternatives to a relatively small number of its students. The term "comprehensive alternative program" is used to describe the less common situation in which the entire school is divided into several alternative programs, with all students enrolled in one or more of the alternatives.

The Limited Alternative Program

Let us first take a closer look at the limited alternative program. As indicated above, such an arrangement typically develops when a large school develops a single alternative program for some designated student population. Limited alternative programs are most often developed for disruptive students, unmotivated and nonachieving students, or talented but alienated students. In each case the school responds to a group of students who are creating problems by developing a special program, usually one designed specifically to meet the supposed needs of the students invited to join.

Limited alternatives have several characteristic features. The teachers are usually self-selected from among the faculty of the parent school. The number of students enrolled is relatively small; one estimate indicated that enrollment in the fifty limited alternatives in Philadelphia averaged about sixty students (personal communication from Leonard Finkelstein, director of the Alternative Program Office in Philadelphia). The schedule is flexible, usually a block-of-time schedule which the staff and students can modify daily. The curriculum often emphasizes basic skills or career awareness. Instruction is often individualized, with extensive use made of active learning strategies. Rules are usually more flexible, although in some limited alternatives developed for disruptive students, there is a strong measure of teacher control.

Such limited alternative programs can be found in almost every metropolitan area. A few will be mentioned briefly here for purposes of illustration.

The Mini-School within Banning High School (Los Angeles) includes one hundred tenth graders whose junior high records suggested that they might experience academic difficulty in high school. Their daily program is built around a flexible schedule and integrates learning in English, science, and mathematics. Extensive use is made of independent study, field trips, and guest speakers.

The Logos program in Seattle is described this way:

> Logos aims at establishing an atmosphere in which each individual has an active voice in how the program functions. Its intent is to give perspective to the conflict of group need versus individual needs, and to establish a commitment on the part of students to making decisions about their learning environment and the resolution of conflicts that may develop. ... A variety of learning strategies, such as reading, writing, observing, debating, confronting, working as an apprentice, and role playing are used to enable the learner to decide how he learns best. Finally the aspect of community responsibility emphasizes the establishment of a supportive relationship between the alternative program and the community in which it is located [Hickey, 1972, p. 14].

Logos includes thirty students from grades 9–12, has one certificated teacher with two noncertificated aides, and is designed to help students reenter the parent high school.

The Concept I Learning Program at Beachwood High School (Ohio) includes a staff of nine teachers and approximately 150 students. The courses of study in Concept I are based upon the needs and interests of students and staff. The instructional program places much stress upon individualization; grades are optional, with student evaluations negotiated monthly between teacher and students.

Focus Project (Portland, Oregon) is an alternative for ninth and tenth graders at the Madison High School who have lost interest in school and are seen as potential dropouts. Focus team members draw up a weekly agenda of activities, field trips, counseling sessions, and laboratory activities, with significant input from students; each Friday the agenda for the coming week is reviewed with the students. And each day the student is able to develop his own schedule. The Focus staff members in cooperation with the students determine how to evaluate the work for that year; no formal report cards are issued.

The Experimental Program of the Oak Park River Forest (Illinois) High School District enrolls 150 high school students who want a nontraditional approach to learning. Most student learning is structured through a student-written learning contract which specifies the subject, the approach to be taken, the resources to be used, and the method of evaluation. Students can use independent study, work–study, or a conventional classroom approach to mastery. A faculty–student senate is the decision-making body for the program. Students are able to use all the facilities of the Oak Park and River Forest High School and the community.

The Content Area Reading Experiences Program of the Gratz High School (Philadelphia, Pennsylvania) offers a work-study program to forty-five poor readers, who have been identified as disruptive pupils and potential dropouts. A linguistics approach to reading forms the basis of instruction in reading, arithmetic, and social studies.

The William Howard Taft Junior High School (San Diego, California) established the Taft Interdisciplinary School (TIS) in the spring of 1970. Physically a part of the Taft school, TIS operates as a semiautonomous unit; its ten teachers and 300 students work together in an interdisciplinary program. Students can enroll in such courses as Wars of the World, Social Simulations, Shakespeare, African History, Minorities, as well as in courses at the regular junior high school.

Even that brief list of representative alternative programs suggests the diversity possible, limited perhaps only by the constraints of the facilities, the budgetary support, and the creativity of the teachers. In each of these instances, the alternative program is limited, as the term is used here, since it serves only a small portion of the students enrolled in the school.

The Comprehensive Alternative Program

The comprehensive alternative program, on the other hand, is a total restructuring of the larger school into several alternative units, with all students involved in making a choice, even when one of those choices is a somewhat conventional school structure.

The alternatives offered as units within the Berkeley High School (California) provide one of the most comprehensive and widely publicized examples. As of 1974, the following units were providing options to the students of Berkeley:

1. Genesis. Originally Community High School, Berkeley's first alternative, Genesis, now enrolls over 160 students. Since its inception in 1969, Community-Genesis has undergone several changes. According to its staff, there is a more general concern for structure because the early "Community High appeared to have gone too far into a 'do-your-own-thing' stance . . . with the stigma of being a 'free, hippie-type' hangout for youths who don't want to work" ("Alternative Education," 1972, p. 19). The program has changed in other ways as well. There is more concern for the basic learning skills and for helping all students get a better sense of other minority groups and cultures.

2. Marcus Garvey Institute. Originally the Other Ways Program developed by Herbert Kohl, Garvey is now a school predominantly of nonwhites, with a curriculum that has a double emphasis of basic learning skills and ethnic awareness.

3. Alliance Black House. This school was started by one of the "tribes" of the early Community High School, which felt that the Community program was too oriented toward white, middle-class values. This description of the program suggests the basic thrust of the school:

> For two hours each morning, these courses are taught: reading and writing, Black studies, general math, Black man and the law, Black literature, chemistry, and political science. The afternoon curriculum includes arts and crafts, geometry, algebra, chemistry, Spanish, Afro Asian dance, Swahili, boxing, biology, and nutritional sciences. Most subjects are offered on a six-week rather than semester basis ["Alternative Education," 1972, p. 8].

As of early 1974, Black House had been temporarily closed by the Justice Department because of "racial segregation."

4. East Campus. Originally part of the high school main campus, East Campus is now located in Savo Island. Its cur-

riculum centers around a work apprenticeship program, operating in the evening for students who need to earn money or have family responsibilities during the day. East Campus strongly believes in an open-door policy: "If a student is dropped from East Campus because he won't show up or won't perform in any way, the door is still open. One student returned after a two-week absence, asked and was granted re-admission, and proceeded to take care of the business of getting the education he needed so there would be a future for him" ("Alternative Education," 1972, p. 16).

5. Model A School. This alternative includes almost 400 students in grades 10–12. All of the program is essentially concerned with the basic skills, with each grade adding its own special emphasis. The tenth grade curriculum, for example, emphasizes the Study of Man; eleventh grade emphasis is on American Culture.

6. Agora. Agora is another alternative with an ethnic focus. Students are equally divided among black, Chicano, white, and Asian. The curriculum has a twofold emphasis— basic skills and community and ethnic awareness. This sketch of the curriculum suggests the thrust of the program:

> Classes at Agora include Harlem Renaissance and what it's like, geometry, language—tool or weapon, Chicano studies, algebra, communication skills, basic design, Black seminar, soccer, modern and Afro dance, math games, art work shop, Black drama, American folklore, creative writing, women's studies, chess, Mexican folk dance, music performance, Spanish, international cooking, human awareness, and tennis ["Alternative Education," 1972, p. 31].

7. School of the Arts. This unit, as its name implies, places central emphasis on the creative and performing arts. In addition to the required courses of math, science, and physical education, the integrated curriculum also includes art, dance, drama, music, television, film making, radio, and communication skills.

8. Berkeley College Preparatory. This unit, enrolling a small group of fifty sophomores and juniors, has a basic college preparatory curriculum with the academic courses taught from

"an Afro-American perspective." Students are taught the skills of test taking.

9. On-Target School. Opened in 1971, On-Target School (OTS) has a career education emphasis. The school conducts frequent field trips to airports, hospitals, banks, plants, and industries. The student takes his academic work at Berkeley High School; OTS provides help in test taking, job counseling, and counseling in specialized occupational areas.

In addition, the Berkeley school system offers numerous junior high and elementary electives. Larry Wells, director of the Experimental Schools Project of the Berkeley Unified School District, indicated that as of March 1974 there were "5000 students enrolled in 25 sub-schools, 20 of them on site at existing campuses and five in leased facilities" (Wells, 1973, pp. 56–57).

Quincy Senior High (Illinois) operates a Title III project called Education by Choice, under which the high school has been restructured into seven alternatives, serving 1,500 students in grades 11 and 12:

1. The Traditional School, as its name implies, is openly committed to a structure and a curriculum that emphasize conventional educational approaches. As the school's booklet indicates, "the Traditional School is designed for those students who desire or need direction, guidance, and supervision to work up to their ability and expectations. The teacher-directed education of the Traditional School provides the best atmosphere for these students to realize their maximum potential" (Haugh, n.d., p. 3). The Traditional School uses a six-period day, with fifty-five minute periods. Students are encouraged to take a full roster of courses, so that unscheduled time is kept to a minimum. Class attendance is stressed. Student evaluation is solely the responsibility of the teacher, who uses the traditional quizzes, papers, and test grades. Achievement is reported with the conventional A, B, C, D, F system.

2. The Flexible School tries to provide a kind of structured flexibility. The schedule is built on twenty twenty-minute modules, with the total amount of class time scheduled for each

subject varying. The Flexible School also emphasizes its adviser–advisee program; each teacher has twenty-two students whom he or she advises on academic and personal matters. The school also places much stress on the community involvement program; students are encouraged to take an active part in community organizations and institutions. One of the most distinctive features of the Flexible School is Flex day. Each Flex day (Wednesday) staff members plan class work that varies from the normal pattern. Most staff members use the day for makeup work, problem-solving sessions, and small group activities. The student on Flex day may follow his regular schedule, choose a meeting with the adviser, work in the community, or go on a field trip.

3. The PIE School (Project to Individualize Education) is considered by school administrators as the "most open" of the alternatives. A PIE student is given the opportunity to take part in a variety of learning situations, including alternatives in course content, out-of-school activities, and sessions with a teacher–adviser. Each teacher schedules himself or herself on a weekly basis. On the basis of course requirements or personal interests, the students schedule themselves into lectures, out-of-school activities, independent study contracts, or discussion groups. Student evaluation is seen as a cooperative effort between student and teacher.

4. The Fine Arts School, as its name implies, places a strong emphasis on visual arts, drama, music. Students with special talents and interests are encouraged to elect this alternative. The staff tries to encourage the students to take an active part in the decision-making process and to participate in off-campus community involvement programs including volunteer work in hospitals, day-care centers, or homes for the elderly.

5. The Career School is designed to assist students in acquiring occupational skills and attitudes. As the school's booklet stresses, "The main objectives of the Career School are to assist students in the attainment of economic independence and the development of an appreciation for the dignity of

work" (Haugh, n.d., p. 11). Many of the Career School students
work at part-time jobs and receive credit for their on-the-job
training through such cooperative programs as Cooperative
Vocational Education, Distributive Education, and Agri-
Business. The student activity program also places a heavy emphasis upon career-related activities. Standard report cards are
issued to inform the student and parents about academic progress.

6. The Work–Study School was designed primarily for
students who seemed dropout prone. Out-of-school jobs, intensive counseling, sheltered work experiences, and an individualized curriculum are provided to help such students develop greater motivation and increase achievement. The
academic subjects offered emphasize vocational orientation,
and prevocational work laboratories stress work habits, attitudes, vocational adjustment, and good appearance. All students are scheduled for two-hour classes in English and history, with the teacher being primarily responsible for communication with the home.

7. Special Education School is designed for students who
require special education services. The school's major goals are
to improve social maturity and vocational competencies, give
the student independent living skills, and help the student develop a realistic self-concept. To meet those goals, the school
has developed a three-phase curriculum which stresses prevocational instruction, practical vocational training, and on-the-
job experience. The work experience program includes on-
campus work for some (jobs in cafeteria, custodial and clerical
jobs) and off-campus community employment.

The Quincy High School alternatives were put into operation with very few problems. After the basic design of the seven
alternatives had been developed, the teachers were given a
chance to indicate first and second choices for their own as-
signments. Then students were told about the proposed alternatives and given an opportunity to make a first and second
choice. Final selections were then made by both teachers and

students (with student choice ratified by parents). Fortunately, teacher and student preferences balanced so well that everyone involved received his or her first or second choice.

Dominican High School in Detroit operates what it calls a quad schedule, where the major differentiation takes place through scheduling options. The schedules and programs offered at Dominican are as follows:

1. *The Structured Schedule* is available for upperclassmen who desire it, and all entering freshmen are assigned to the Structured Schedule. Under the Structured Schedule, all students attend either classes or a directed study center. For the first month an orientation program is built into the schedule and is used to help freshmen develop the skills of self-directed learning. At the beginning of the second quarter of the school year, freshmen who indicate willingness and readiness are able to move out of the structured program.

2. *The Modular Schedule* is designed for sophomores, juniors, and seniors who prefer the option of arranging their own unscheduled time (which ranges from 30 to 60 percent of total school time) and who want to do regular academic work in small groups or independently. The Modular Schedule is similar to the Flexible Schedule of Quincy in terms of the degree of structure provided.

3. *The Open Schedule* is available to upperclassmen who prefer more openness. According to the school's bulletin, the Open Schedule is designed for students who "want an environment which is based on a personal approach to learning, wish to identify and pursue their individual goals and interests, are self-motivated, are willing to assume responsibility for their own education, seek to manage their own time and resources, wish to pursue independent learning as an integral dimension of the total approach to learning, seek to expand their formal education in the pursuit of lifelong learning" ("The Quad Scheduling Program," 1974, p. 2). Students in the Open Schedule meet weekly in a small "home-base" group with a faculty coordinator to share learning experiences. They also

have access to the Open Schedule Resource Center, a common room where students and faculty meet for discussions, work in informal groups, and pursue individual projects. The program stresses extensive student involvement in independent learning approaches.

4. *The Alternative School* emphasizes an experiential approach to learning, with most of the students involved in internships and work experiences. Here a home-base group is also used for planning and sharing the results of learning. The home-base group meets daily with a teacher–facilitator, who helps students find a focus for their work. Students can use the Alternative School Resource Center for individual discussions and projects. The Alternative School places a heavy emphasis upon developing group cohesiveness and enhancing personal development.

Principal Dan Hogan indicates that the Modular Schedule school was the most appealing to the students, enrolling close to 80 percent of them; the Open Schedule enrolled about 10 percent, as did the Alternative School (reported in telephone conversation, May 1974). Students and parents receive extensive orientation before they select a schedule. One sign of the success of the Structured Schedule is that by the end of the first quarter all freshmen are able to move into a less structured program, with some qualifying for open campus privileges.

One final example of the comprehensive alternative program is the Haaren High School in New York City. The Haaren School, which enrolls close to 2,000 students, is divided into twelve mini-schools. Each mini-school has a specific objective or program thrust, with emphasis on such areas as aerospace, urban affairs, business, and creative arts. Each mini-school has a head teacher, with three or four additional teachers for a student population of 125–150 students. Teaching teams are self-contained; a given team is responsible for the instruction of only its students. Each teaching team also has a street worker, a young man who serves as liaison between the students' homes and the teachers.

A Recommended Alternative Program

Initial reports from all four comprehensive alternative programs indicate success in mitigating the negative effects of bigness and in reaching the students served. On the basis of this success and his own commitment to diversity and pluralism, the author recommends that large schools move toward a program of comprehensive alternative programs. The author would first like to describe the nature of the alternatives he believes should be offered and then suggest a planning process for their establishment.

What types of alternative programs should a school offer? Since the author believes in local planning, he is convinced that this question must finally be answered by the schools themselves. To assist in such planning, however, he would like to make some recommendations concerning the types to be considered. In considering types of alternative programs, one could simply replicate the types of alternative schools identified in Chapter 2 (student-centered, program-centered, place-centered). However, the author feels that alternative programs inside the comprehensive school present special problems involving the students', staff's, and parents' attitude, so that not all of the types of alternative schools would make desirable alternative programs. The author does not want to stigmatize any student or to perpetuate undesirable stratification, and would therefore reject programs that are explicitly offered for a given type of student (such as gifted, disruptive, or drug-habituated). And since the programs operate within the school, for the most part, differentiation by place is also inappropriate. Obviously, some other approach to a typology is necessary.

In developing typology for program options, the author feels the two most significant dimensions should be (1) environment, the degree of openness and structure, and (2) curriculum, the central thrust of the school's offerings. Neither environmental differentiation nor curricula options

Table 3 Seven Alternative Programs

Type	Probable Enrollment
Traditional	500
Flexible	800
Alternative	200
Free	50
Career	150
Creative Arts	150
Cultural awareness	150
Total	2,000

would necessarily stigmatize those enrolling in the different programs, and a large, previously conventional school should be able to provide both. Based upon the size of the school and the special nature of the student population, the initial design for the comprehensive alternative program should include three or four programs that vary significantly in environment and two to four that vary in terms of curricula thrust.

For a typical comprehensive school in the city or suburbs, four programs are recommended that have an environmental option (traditional, flexible, alternative, free) and three that have a curricula option (career, creative arts, cultural awareness). In a school of 2,000 these seven alternative programs would probably attract the numbers of students shown in Table 3, based upon the author's and others' experience.

What are these programs like? To a great extent, they will take the shape and form desired by their members. However, some of the general characteristics that might develop can be described. Table 4 summarizes the most significant elements; the brief descriptions below indicate the flavor of the program.

Environmental Options

Four options are recommended under the rubric of environmental options. While the significant variable here is the

Table 4 Seven Proposed Alternatives for a School of 2,000 Students

Program	Approximate Enrollment	Environment	Decision Making	Curriculum	Schedule	Space	Teaching	Grading
Traditional	500	Closed	Director	Academic subjects	Period	Classroom	Lecture, recitation	Letter grades
Flexible	800	Moderately structured	Director, with staff and student input	Humanities, mini-courses	Modular	Large-group seminar rooms, resource center	Lecture, discussion, individual study	Letter grades, with pass-fail option
Alternative	200	Open	Teachers, with student input	Broad fields, mini-courses	College	Seminar rooms, community	Discussion	Pass-fail or credit
Free	50	Free	Consensus	Unplanned projects	None	Community	Facilitator	None
Career	150	Structured	Director, with staff and student input	Careers	Modular	School, community	Master craftsman	Letter grades, with pass-fail option
Creative arts	150	Open	Teachers, students	Creativity	Block of time	Studios	Artist	Pass-fail
Cultural Awareness	150	Moderately structured	Director	Cultural awareness	Modular	Seminar rooms	Ethnic model	Letter grades, with pass-fail option

climate or environment, in a given kind of environment such matters as curriculum, schedule, and grading are in consonance with each other. The period schedule, for example, seems to fit a traditional school; the modular schedule, a flexible school; and so on.

Traditional. The traditional program tries to retain the best of the past. It is provided for the student who needs and prefers maximum structure. The environment might best be described as "closed" or "highly structured." There are very specific rules governing student conduct: no smoking, no lateness, no cutting, no roaming the halls. Discipline is rather strictly enforced, with suspension, detention, and expulsion meted out to offenders. The decisions are made by the director, who makes no pretense of wanting extensive student or staff involvement in governance. The curriculum is a standard academic curriculum organized by conventional subjects. Students meet in groups of 25–35 for forty-five-minute periods for instruction. Instructional space is not differentiated, all classrooms being for general purposes. Most of the teaching is didactic presentation, followed by recitation. Conventional letter grades are used. While the traditional school is roundly scored as being unimaginative, it appeals to students and teachers who like a structured environment, and every adult knows from his or her own experience that some exciting teaching and learning can occur in conventional classrooms.

Flexible. The flexible program resembles the "innovative" schools of the sixties. It is provided for students who want structure with flexibility. The environment might best be described as "moderately structured." Rules requiring class attendance and prohibiting smoking in the building are closely enforced. However, students may move from resource center to class without a hall pass, and there is a lounge area where students can talk quietly and move about. Decisions are made by the director in consultation with teachers and with student input. The curriculum includes many "humanities" offerings and several mini-courses in the English and social studies areas. The program uses a modular schedule, and extensive use is made of large-group and small-group instruction; independent study time is provided for students to work in resource centers. Teachers vary lecture with small-group discussion, supplemented with independent study projects. Letter grades with pass-fail options are used. The flexible program would probably have the greatest appeal to secondary school students; it has the combination of structure and openness that most seem to prefer.

Alternative Program. The alternative program looks like many of the alternative schools now operating. It is provided for students who want a great deal of freedom with some measure of adult structuring. The environment might best be described as "open." There are only a few rules, which are enforced by peer pressure, with expulsion as an extreme threat for only those who insist on defying the few rules. Real power is held by the teaching staff, with significant input from the students. The alternative program's curriculum is organized primarily in a "broad fields" approach, with some use of minicourses; the courses are primarily student-centered and concerned with timely and "relevant" issues. The schedule is a "college" or "arena" schedule; students make their own schedules and are required to be in school only when scheduled for class. Most classes meet in small seminar rooms, although extensive use is made of the community for community-based learning. Most classes provide a teacher-led discussion. "Pass-fail" or "credits" are used for grades. The alternative program is a good one for those students who want a new kind of learning experience but are not ready for the radical experimentation of the free school.

Free Program. The free program resembles the free schools which were so widely publicized in the late sixties. It is provided for students who want the maximum amount of freedom and openness. The environment is described as "free" in a Summerhillian sense. There are no rules, except those which develop on an ad hoc basis. Decisions are made on the basis of consensus, with the whole group deliberating about important issues. There is no curriculum in the sense of planned courses;

people meet and decide together which project will occupy
them—dome building, political protest, experimental drama.
There is no schedule; people agree to meet at an appointed time
and to work out problems of time and space. Extensive use is
made of the community; in fact, the community is the primary
place for learning. The teacher does not see himself or herself
as "teacher," only as facilitator and an equal participant. No
grades or evaluations are given; a diploma is awarded when the
student feels he or she is ready to graduate. The free program
should appeal to a small number of students who in fact want
to transcend the role of student.

Curriculum Options

There are three curriculum options that would most appeal
to secondary school students. While certain types of scheduling and environments seem appropriate for each type of program, there is less consistency across the several dimensions
with these program options than there were with environmental options.

Career Program. The career program has as its central mission helping young people explore a variety of careers and
develop a deeper understanding of themselves and the careers
they can best follow. And "career" is used in its broadest sense;
the young people in this program explore and try out a variety
of professional, technical, and managerial careers. The environment is probably best described as "structured"; there is a
direct and open type of adult control, but it is not authoritarian.
The decisions are probably made by the director, with teacher
and student input. The curriculum, of course, focuses on career
awareness, career exploration, and career specialization. Yet
that emphasis on careers is related to concerns for self-
awareness and academic competency. The schedule is a flexible modular schedule to provide the longer blocks of time
necessary for career-oriented workshops. Large, open-space
areas are provided for student projects, but extensive use is
made of the community—factories, shopping centers, offices.
There are many community-based apprenticeships of all sorts;

students spend time working side by side with physicians, attorneys, retail store managers, architects, musicians, plumbers, and tree surgeons. Much of the instruction is project-centered; the teacher acts as a master craftsman with the apprentice. The student is evaluated in terms of his or her mastery of specific competencies. Obviously, the career school should attract many young people who are job- and achievement-oriented.

Creative Arts Program. The creative arts program is concerned with creative making, creative thinking, creative being. It is designed to appeal to students who have a variety of talents—musical, theatrical, verbal, mechanical, artistic—and who want to work in an open atmosphere developing those creative talents. The environment is very open, with a minimum of structure; the students are so involved in creative production that rules seem unnecessary, except for a few commonsense guidelines. Decisions are made by teachers and students in an atmosphere of open discussion. The curriculum is oriented entirely toward creativity. Special courses are offered in all types of creative thinking and problem solving —Synectics, morphological analysis, lateral thinking, brainstorming. And there are studio workshops of all sorts in which students learn how to create with metal, fabric, wood, paint, clay, words, music. The schedule is an open, block-of-time schedule to provide the longer work periods necessary for creative production. There are large open-space workshops and studios and a large theater. The teachers function as artists and producers, demonstrating their own creativity and inspiring the young people to create on their own. All grades are pass-fail.

Cultural Awareness. The cultural awareness program is designed to appeal to all students who seem to gain their primary identity through their special culture. It is not just a school for blacks; hopefully the program will attract several ethnic groups—Jews, blacks, Chicanos, Orientals, Italians, Polish, Irish, and so on. The environment is moderately structured, since most of the students enrolled prefer an environment where there is more adult direction and less "fooling around."

Decisions are made by a strong director, with input from teachers and students. The curriculum, of course, is the major element; its central focus is on the concept of culture and on an understanding of the several cultures represented. Students spend one-third of their day studying culture from a social- and physical-science point of view, one-third of their day studying their own culture in classes grouped according to ethnic identity, and one-third studying the other cultures represented in the school. A flexible modular schedule is used, with much use of small-group seminars. While the school is the primary center of learning, a real effort is made to bring the community into the school and to take the students out into the community to see people of different cultures living in their own special milieu. Teachers are chosen on the basis of their own ethnic awareness, and they make a real effort to keep in balance their ethnic awareness and their commitment to the larger society. Standard letter grades are given, with some pass-fail options.

A Recommended Calendar for Planning

Hopefully, Table 4 and the text together suggest to school administrators some of the varieties possible in alternative programs. How can such programs be implemented without undue difficulty? The author prefers a simple planning model built upon maximum participation of all those involved, yet designed to accomplish the goals with efficiency and effectiveness. Such an approach to planning is outlined in Table 5. Perhaps a few comments about it are in order.

First, the idea for alternative programs begins when someone decides it makes sense. That someone can be a school administrator, a teacher or group of teachers, a group of students, or a group of parents. Change can begin anyplace.

The idea is presented in outline form to the board and the chief school administrator for review. A decision should be made quickly to avoid the frustration and cynicism that develop when an administrator tries to stall by telling a group to

Table 5 Planning Calendar for Alternative Programs

Month	Task	Primarily Responsible
December	Some individual or group decides school should offer alternative programs.	Administrator, teachers, students, parents
January	Decision is made to go ahead with planning; policy constraints and general resources identified.	Board and chief school administrator
February	Planning task force appointed for entire project; task force makes needs assessment.	Chief school administrator with school principal
March	Broad list of tentative programs developed, each with its own environment, program, goals.	Task force with principal
	Staff is oriented to alternative programs and expresses initial preference.	School principal
	Students and parents are oriented.	School principal
April	Students express initial preferences.	Principal, staff
	Final decision made on programs to be offered.	Chief administrator, principal
May	Teachers and students make final choices.	Principal
	Final assignment of teachers and students made.	Principal
	Director for each program selected.	Chief administrator, principal
	Budget and space allocations made.	Chief administrator, principal
June	Planning groups for each program make preliminary decisions.	Director with groups
September	Programs begin.	
November	Problem-solving workshops held.	Director

study an idea for a year and then after a year's study tells the
group that it is just not feasible. Hopefully, the board and the
chief school administrator will give approval, identify the
broad policy constraints within which all programs must operate, and allocate special personnel and fiscal resources.

With general approval received, a planning task force
composed of the school principal, and selected teachers, parents, students, and community representatives is appointed.
The planning task force is responsible only for the early stages
of planning, not for the intensive and detailed planning of the
later stages. The task force makes a needs assessment: it surveys a sample of students and parents; it surveys the entire
faculty; it gathers data about other comprehensive alternative
programs; it assembles data about the students' achievements,
abilities, and interests. On the basis of this needs assessment,
the task force develops a tentative list of perhaps ten programs,
with brief descriptions of their environments, programs, and
general goals.

At that point the building principal assumes major responsibility for the planning. He or she orients the entire staff to the
general concept of the comprehensive alternative programs and
to the specific nature of each choice. Every teacher is asked to
state a tentative first and second choice for his or her teaching
assignment. Then students and parents are fully informed
about the program through bulletins, large-group sessions, and
small-group discussions. In these orientation sessions the principal stresses that everyone's choice will be honored and that
such choices are never completely final. Students are then
polled as to their preliminary preferences.

Based upon the preliminary data on teachers' and students'
preferences, the chief school administrator and the school
principal together make a policy decision about the types of
alternatives to be offered. Teachers and students are then asked
to make a final choice, indicating a first and second choice.
Based upon these final tallies, the principal and staff determine
final placement of teachers and students.

With final enrollments determined, the chief school administrator and the principal select a director for each program,

and make a final decision on budget and space allocated to each program. At that point the director for each program organizes for that program a number of planning groups, who meet during June (and possibly the summer months) to make tentative decisions on such matters as curriculum, materials, schedule—all those matters that must be settled in advance.

The school year opens with planning workshops that involve all participants. Under the leadership of specialists in group dynamics, staff and students are involved in community-building exercises. They then begin to work in small groups on such matters as grading policies, parent involvement, community participation, public relations, student activities, rules and limits, and sanctions.

The programs begin operation. After a shakedown period of eight weeks, regular instruction is halted in all programs and in a three-day workshop students, parents, and teachers evaluate the program, identify problems, develop tentative solutions, and make plans for improvement.

Through such a planning process, one large school has become transformed into seven alternative programs, each with its own dynamic thrust.

References

"Alternative Education," Berkeley, California: Experimental Schools Program, October 1972.

"Directory of Alternative Public Schools," *Changing Schools*, n.d., No. 8.

Friedenberg, Edgar Z. "If You're an Elephant . . ." in *High School*, edited by Ronald Gross and Paul Osterman. New York: Simon and Schuster, 1971.

Hansen, Ralph. "Are Optional Public Alternatives Viable?" *Changing Schools*, 1973.

Haugh, Richard. "Education by Choice." Quincy, Illinois: Quincy Senior High II School District, n.d.

Hickey, Mike. *Alternative Education*. Seattle, Washington: Seattle School District, 1972.

"Quad Scheduling Program, The," Detroit: Dominican High School, 1974.

Wells, Larry. "Options in a Small District: Berkeley," *NASSP Bulletin*, September 1973, pp. 55–60.

CHAPTER FOUR

Alternative
Paths
Previous chapters suggested that alternative
schools and programs can provide viable options for most of
the students through a comprehensive restructuring of the
school and its program. For those school systems not yet ready
for such comprehensive change, alternative paths can be a useful way of providing alternatives for individual students. This
chapter examines the concept of alternative paths, defends the
need for such programs, discusses implementation strategies,
describes briefly the types of paths available, suggests a simple
planning process, and indicates some special problems which
must be confronted if the idea of paths is to succeed.

Alternative Paths—The Concept and the Need

As explained in Chapter 1, the term "alternative path" is used
here to mean a system by which the school or school system
makes it possible for individual students to study and earn
diploma credits through a variety of external learning experiences. Whereas the development of alternative schools and
programs requires the restructuring of the organization and is
concerned primarily with organizational changes, the alternative path focuses on individual students and the guidance and
administrative arrangements necessary for a student to learn
and earn credits through nonschool approaches. Such

nonschool approaches, as we shall observe later, can include a variety of diverse activities such as correspondence study, watching television, independent study at home, and taking courses offered by community-based groups.

Why are such arrangements necessary? There are two arguments for such an approach—one organizational; the other, individual.

The organizational argument is that some school systems feel they are not ready for the more comprehensive changes required for alternative schools or programs. There may be insufficient student interest, a lack of staff readiness, or too much community resistance to such sweeping changes. The alternative path approach meets all such objections: it can provide for only one student, if necessary; it does not require extensive staff support; and it can be implemented without the undue publicity that would arouse community antagonism.

The other argument focuses on the individual student whose needs are not being served by the conventional school. For a variety of reasons, many of these students do not want to attend an alternative school or program. They are students for whom "school" and its attendant associations with buildings, organizations, and crowds are simply dysfunctional and inhibiting.

Who are such students? Several types come readily to mind:

1. Gifted, independent youth. These are very mature students who are so gifted and autonomous that they prefer to learn in a totally independent mode outside the school. Often they are so far advanced in their thinking and divergent in their life-style that they do not relate to their age-mates but prefer to live in the adult world. One young person of this writer's acquaintance was able to earn two years of high school credit in one year of independent study, went to work full-time in public radio, and at age eighteen had his own program and was working as a "stringer" for several daily newspapers.

2. Pregnant girls. While most pregnant girls should probably stay in school—either a regular or an alternative school

—there are some who, for a variety of reasons, might do better on an alternative path. In some cases their physical health is such that school attendance is unwise. In some cases their emotional adjustment to the pregnancy is so poor that, for a while at least, they do not want extensive contact with peers. And in a few cases conditions at home are such that their presence is required.

3. Disruptive students. Some students find any institutional setting so intolerable that they find themselves in constant conflict with schools. While alternative schools have been able to reduce the institutional pressures for many such students, some find even the alternative school environment too restrictive and authoritarian. Such students have extreme difficulty accepting any kind of authority or dealing with any group of peers. Often they can be helped, at least on an interim basis, through an alternative path that builds an individual program to meet their needs.

4. Dropouts and potential dropouts. It is estimated that one-fourth of all high school students drop out of school each year at an annual cost to the nation of $6 billion (Levin, 1972). Such dropouts and potential dropouts can be readily identified. According to one study, the following characteristics are typical: inability to read at grade level, pattern of failure in school, withdrawal from extracurricular activity, disruption in classroom, frequent absenteeism, weak peer relationships in school, and emotional disturbance related to home environment (National School Public Relations Association, 1972). Although most schools try to develop several types of ad hoc arrangements for such students, the students still drop out of school for work, marriage, or a life of drifting.

5. Young veterans. Of 5 million men discharged from military service in the last several years, about 750,000 lacked a high school diploma (Bailey, Macy, and Vickers, 1973). Many of these veterans would be receptive to enrolling in a school which is able and willing to provide the resources for them to complete their high school diplomas through an out-of-school path.

There are many other students, of course, who do not fit these categories and could still benefit from some alternative path. Children of migrant workers, young people involved with drugs and excluded from school, handicapped youth who are not being helped by existing programs, and young parents who have not completed high school—all would constitute the target population.

Such youth, of course, are eligible for two existing approaches to out-of-school learning, but neither is working quite satisfactorily. One is the High School Equivalency Diploma, a diploma awarded to youth and adults who make the requisite scores on achievement tests. However, this program has not been too successful in reaching the youth identified here. The main problem is that most states restrict the equivalency program to older youth; regulations typically provide that a person can take the test only after he or she has reached age nineteen; young people between seventeen and nineteen can take the test only if they have been out of school for a year or if their high school class has graduated. Another problem is that a large proportion fail the tests. For example, in 1971 only 51 percent of those taking the tests made a passing grade (Bailey, Macy, and Vickers, 1973, p. 30).

The other approach which has had mixed success is homebound tutoring. While homebound instruction seems to have worked effectively with many young people, it is not always the best solution. To begin with, it is a costly program for school districts. In Philadelphia, for example, a teacher for the homebound earning $900 monthly and working full time is expected to teach only ten students a week.

A second problem at the high school level is that the teacher for the homebound is often expected to instruct in all subjects in the standard curriculum. The teacher, for example, who has majored in English is sometimes called upon to teach science, mathematics, and foreign languages.

Finally, homebound instruction is still conventional instruction, relying on a teacher using a conventional mode of instruction. Many students who are having trouble in school or

have been expelled have difficulty relating to conventional
teachers and in understanding standard textbooks.

For these students, some new approach is needed. Alternative paths might be the answer.

Implementation and Operation

How would the alternative paths operate? One excellent model
has been proposed by the Policy Institute of the Syracuse University Research Corporation.

Under the Syracuse plan, a regional learning service is set
up to serve the target population of a multi-county region. The
regional learning service provides each adult or youth desiring
an alternative path with a learning consultant, a part-time
salaried educational counselor. The learning consultant diagnoses the applicant's skills and reviews the past record to determine what the learner can do and what he or she needs to
learn to receive the high school diploma. Two important access
tools are available to the learning consultant and the
learner: (1) an educational resource directory, a computerized
information bank identifying eleven school-based and out-of-
school learning resources, and (2) a regional instructional reserve, a talent bank of tutors approved for servicing the learner.
The learning consultant and the learner together draw up a
plan of study leading to the external diploma. It is proposed
that in each school district a validation panel, composed of
teachers and specially qualified outsiders, be set up. The validation panel would review the test data and portfolio of each
learner, following completion of the plan of study, and determine if he or she is qualified for the external diploma.

As of the writing of this work, the Syracuse plan had begun
to operate on a pilot basis in New York State. (For a full description of the Syracuse plan, see Bailey, Macy, and Vickers, 1973.)
The Syracuse plan has been developed to serve youth and
adults on a regional basis; its use of computerized retrieval
systems and special personnel make it more expensive than

perhaps a local district could afford. However, any school system could use the basic elements of the plan in a locally developed model that would not require additional costs. One such system might operate as follows:

A young person decides he or she wants an alternative path. The initial impetus might come from learner, school administrator, classroom teacher, counselor, parent, or community worker. The learner reports to a member of the school's counseling staff, an alternative learning counselor, trained in diagnosis and counseling in nontraditional study. The learner brings along a simple form indicating tentative parental approval for the alternative path application.

The counselor and the learner spend a few hours together in a diagnostic and planning session. The counselor gives some simple aptitude and achievement tests (if recent data are not available), reviews the learner's previous academic record, discusses preferred learning style and media, probes for future goals, and determines immediate objectives.

The counselor assists the learner in using the school's learning resource file to identify the educational resources needed. As will be described below, the learning resource file is a locally developed file which identifies all the personnel and material resources available in that community.

Based on the learner's needs, his or her educational goals, and the resources identified, the counselor and the learner develop an alternative path contract. The contract specifies the areas of study, the resources to be used, mutually agreed on checkup dates, a proposal for final evaluation, and school credits to be awarded if the evaluation gives satisfactory results.

This learning contract is then signed by the learner, the parents, the counselor, and the school principal.

The learner begins to move on the alternative path identified. He or she meets with the counselor at the times specified in the contract. On a periodic basis the learner meets with a peer support group, a group of age-mates also working on alternative paths. An adult volunteer serves as group convener and facilitator.

When the learner has completed the alternative path agreed upon, he or she meets with an alternative path evaluation panel. The panel is composed of a student, a teacher, and a community representative who has competency in one of the areas in which the learner has concentrated. The evaluation panel meets with the learner and the counselor, reviews the contract, examines a portfolio which the learner has assembled, interviews the learner, and performs other evaluations to determine if the contract has in fact been filled.

Such a locally operated approach can, without additional expense, provide for many young people a variety of alternative paths to the high school diploma. And the types of paths available are numerous and varied.

Types of Paths Available

First, the alternative path approach should encourage the revival of the time-tested apprenticeship way of learning. Apprenticeships have long been used—and should continue to be used—in such crafts as plumbing, pipe fitting, and brick laying. However, the apprenticeship idea need not be limited to such crafts. The idea could be extended to all the professions. A young person could apprentice himself or herself to a teacher, doctor, lawyer, architect, engineer, sculptor, or interior designer. Such professional apprenticeships would not, of course, develop professional competencies but would help the young person explore a career interest, test the reality of the commitment, and gain firsthand knowledge of the profession. Most craftsmen and professional people would be willing to work with a responsible and interested young person who wanted to learn through firsthand experience. Manual High School in Denver, Colorado, has had such professional apprenticeships available for several years now.

The alternative path could also legitimize a variety of tutoring experiences. Many young people who cannot profit from group instruction in the classroom can learn readily from individual tutoring. Mary Kohler and her associates have, in fact, shown that young people can tutor each other with great success (Gartner, Kohler, Riessman, 1971).

A young person might also use an alternative path as a way of getting credit for courses taken through some nonschool agency. Most community colleges and four-year institutions will permit young people to audit selected courses without payment. Almost every community has some kind of adult evening school which offers a variety of courses that would meet the needs of youth on alternative paths. Also, many cities and suburban areas have art centers where instruction in the fine and visual arts is provided.

The media also provide an excellent resource for learners on an alternative path. Every season public television offers some types of college courses for credit. Although video cassettes are not presently available for widespread distribution, many experts in the field predict that they soon will be available on a mass basis. Several companies now offer excellent collections of audio cassettes which contain lectures by such authorities as Carl Rogers, Erich Fromm, and Rollo May for students interested in studying psychology. And under a grant from the National Endowment for the Humanities, selected newspapers are offering courses in American history and civilization.

Correspondence study is another time-honored mode of learning which can be revitalized through alternative paths. Many technical institutes and colleges offer correspondence courses in a variety of fields. (See, for example, such directories as *Guide to Independent Study Through Correspondence Instruction*, and *Directory of Independent Study Programs*.) A guided program in correspondence study now in operation in Bucks County, Pennsylvania, has students working on their correspondence courses in groups under a counselor's direction.

Another readily available resource for independent learning on an alternative path is represented in the thousands of Learning Activity Packages developed by local school systems.

Such LAPs or Unipacks, as they are sometimes called, are teacher-produced materials designed for self-paced and self-directed learning. If the local school does not have its own packages, some knowledgeable teacher can probably identify a nearby district which would have them in the subject needed. The Teachers Unipack Exchange in Salt Lake City, Utah, makes learning packages available at nominal cost.

A variety of community service projects, travel experiences, and work experiences could also help the young person earn academic credit as an alternative path. These options will be discussed more fully in a later chapter; they are mentioned briefly here only as examples of experiential paths.

Many types of voluntary service opportunities exist in every community and provide an excellent learning experience. Some of the ways young people are gaining experience, as well as making a major contribution, include assisting in political campaigns, teaching in nursery schools, helping in a home for the aged, working in municipal offices, organizing community clean-up campaigns, and increasing community awareness of pollution problems.

While travel has always been viewed as "broadening," it has been awarded academic credit only as part of expensive "study tours," in which the so-called study is often limited to a few perfunctory seminars. But travel can be educational—and worthy of academic credit—without being expensive. With the necessary parental approval and support, a young person could plan an itinerary confined to his or her own geographical area, with a specific educational focus. Such a focus could include, for example:

1. Alternative forms of higher education in New England.
2. Art museums and artists' colonies in the Midwest.
3. The history of the Texas Panhandle.
4. Architecture in the Bay Area.
5. Dialect field studies in the Middle Atlantic states.
6. Folk art and crafts in Appalachia.

Students in the Alternative Schools Project in suburban Philadelphia rented a large camping vehicle and made several educational tours across the country (Glatthorn and Briskin, 1973).

Several schools have organized school-to-school exchange programs to eliminate living costs and provide for some kind of local school support. One of the most extensive has been operating at the Cherry Creek High School in Colorado for several years now.

Finally, work experiences of many sorts can constitute a useful alternative path for many youth. Too often work–study plans have been limited to working-class youth, who typically have been working at part-time jobs for years and thus already know about the world of work from firsthand experience. We are suggesting here that under the alternative paths approach, work experience for academic credit be provided for all young people who want it. It would seem especially important for middle-class youth who are having difficulty with school to confront at firsthand the reality of the workaday world.

A Suggested Planning Process

Planning for alternative paths should be relatively simple. First, the chief school administrator should receive approval from the state's department of education. Many states now have policy statements recommending such alternative paths; others will readily approve any sound proposal designed to meet the special needs of the groups identified. The administrator should then receive official board approval of a policy sanctioning the alternative paths concept and structures.

With such approvals received, the chief administrator should then appoint a member of the staff to assume primary responsibility for coordinating the program. While such coordination might ultimately require a full-time commitment from some individual, at the outset it would be wise to assign the task to some present member of the administrative staff. The author's recommendation would be to assign the job to the director of guidance or the assistant principal responsible for curriculum and instruction.

At that stage an advisory council should be established, with significant representation from the community, since the program will require extensive community involvement. In addition, the advisory council should include students, parents, teachers, and school administrators. The advisory council should advise the program's director, propose ideas for implementation, and assist in the critical step of locating resources. As soon as the advisory council has been established, the faculty members should be fully informed about the program, and their ideas should be solicited.

The director of the alternative paths program should then publicize the program extensively throughout the community, emphasizing the identification of resources and the recruitment of participants. The publicity program is so essential that all media should be employed. Flyers from the school, news stories for local and city dailies, spot announcements for radio, and posters placed in supermarkets and shopping centers—all these could be used to get the information to the largest number of people.

At this juncture the director should begin to develop the learning resources file. As previously explained, this file will be instrumental in helping the student find the personnel and material resources to assist him or her along the alternative path. Each school can develop its own particular form for the file. Schools that have the capability might store the information in a computer. Others might prefer to use an edge-punched card that can be needle-sorted to locate different types of resources. The simplest approach is to use six-by-nine-inch index cards, with entry headings and other information mimeographed on the cards.

Each card should contain spaces in which the following information can be entered:

Subject area, skill, or competency
Name of resource
Address
Telephone number

Contact person
Description of resource
Fee or cost
Information concerning availability
Directions for retrieving resource
Brief evaluation of resource by users

With these forms prepared, the director should then instruct clerical help in how to locate all possible resources. As pointed out before, the learning resource file will list people of various sorts: tutors, senior citizens with special competencies, artists, craftsmen, teachers, physicians, engineers, architects, merchants, business executives—anyone interested in assisting a young person with his or her education. The file should list educational institutions—art museums, adult schools, YMCA's, community centers, churches and synagogues—and all the courses offered by those institutions. It should list all media resources—books, newspapers, television courses, cassette tapes. It should include all correspondence courses. It is a complete storehouse of all the resources available for independent learning.

The next step is to identify and train the alternative learning counselor who will specialize in alternative path counseling. As will be pointed out in the next section, these learning counselors will provide key linkages in the program. They should be selected for their knowledge of alternative learning approaches and their ability to relate to the target population. If the district can support some special training, they should be given the opportunity to read widely in the field of alternative study, to visit programs currently underway, and to consult with people experienced in working with out-of-school youth and in developing programs for them.

The next stage in the planning process would be to develop specific procedures, policies, and forms necessary to implement the program successfully. The forms needed would include a letter explaining the program to interested adults who want to volunteer their services, a questionnaire to be

completed by the adult or the institution supplying the learning resource (this information will later be transferred to an
index card), the permission form to be signed by the parent, a
letter explaining the program to the interested student, the
learning contract which the student will complete with the
learning counselor as a map showing the alternative path, and
an evaluation report to be completed by the validation panel. In
addition to all these forms, it is recommended that an outline of
policies and procedures be stated in a short booklet which
can be distributed to all applicants and to other interested parties.

The final stage is to begin the recruiting of participants.
Most of the effective recruiting will have to be done through
telephoning and personal meetings, since the alienated out-of-
school young person is not often reached by letters, posters,
and other announcements. All teachers should be encouraged
to take part in the recruiting process, and the counseling staff
will, of course, play a critical role.

So the program should be ready. Problems will develop
—and those are the concern of the final section in this discussion.

Solving Problems Through Evaluation,
the Counselor, and the Group

The openness, flexibility, and individuality of the alternative
path approach are all strengths which commend it to school
administrators for serious consideration. However, these same
strengths will inevitably produce some serious problems that
seem entirely predictable. After identifying these problems, the
author would like to suggest ways of dealing with them.

To begin with, some students will try to cut corners in
completing their learning contracts. They will be tempted to
list books they have not read, report conferences they did not
attend, and request credit for correspondence courses they did
not complete.

Some students will attempt to do too much in too short a period. Often older students out of school for a few years will become overconfident in their ability to do the high school work they now consider "kid stuff."

Other students will lose their motivation to continue with the program. They will begin with an initial burst of enthusiasm but then find that independent study outside of school is a very difficult way to learn.

There will be other problems of lesser moment. There will be some initial faculty resistance. There will be some difficulties with record keeping. And some colleges and employers may resist accepting nontraditional learning credits.

But the major problems will be with the learner, and these must be confronted and dealt with. Three important elements of the alternative path proposal will deal with them: the evaluation system, the alternative learning counselor, and the peer support group.

1. The evaluation system is a critical element. It is important to develop an evaluation system that is legitimate and cannot be faked, is fair to the learner and not a frustrating hurdle, and is flexible enough to accommodate nontraditional study.

The author thinks the evaluation system proposed here has important components which will assure that it meets those criteria. First, the evaluation system should be self-initiated. The student should propose the manner in which the work will be evaluated. The alternative learning counselor will assist the student in proposing an evaluation process that makes sense in terms of the learning task and the student's method of completing that task, but it will be the student's job essentially to identify the evaluation procedure and instruments. Making the student assume this responsibility of identifying the evaluation process will help him or her to think more critically about the level of competency to be reached and the means of assessing that competency.

Second, insofar as possible the evaluation process should be competency-based. The evaluation should require that the student demonstrate that he or she has the competency specified. The length of time it took to acquire that competency or the manner in which it was acquired should be irrelevant. If a student has learned to speak and read French by living abroad for one year and has achieved the competency expected of a third-year student of French, the student should receive credit for three years of French. If a student can demonstrate that he or she can read, write, and speak English with the competency expected of a senior English student, the English requirement should be considered satisfied.

Third, the way in which the competencies are evaluated should be individualized.

How can competencies be evaluated? Several standardized examinations are available, such as the various College Entrance Examination Board tests and subject-achievement tests published by major publishers. In addition, each school should begin to develop its own collection of end-of-year examinations, with the best of these reviewed and improved by consultants in testing and evaluation. Some competencies can be demonstrated simply in a brief oral examination: the ability to type or take dictation; the ability to make a brief extemporaneous speech; the ability to speak fluent French. Other competencies can be demonstrated through some final product: a poem, a piece of sculpture, a musical composition, a design for a dress, a handcrafted table or chair. And some competencies can be certified by a professional or craftsman who has supervised the student at work: a teacher can certify that the teacher aide has certain instructional competencies; a shop supervisor can certify that a young man or woman can in fact operate a lathe. The student will be assisted in choosing an individualized evaluation system which will best reflect the nature of the learning and most validly assess the competency.

Finally, the evaluation should be performed by some group external to the instructional process. Too often in school the one who does the teaching also does the testing; the teacher thus often becomes the judge and then the adversary, and such relationships are antithetical to a good teacher–student relationship. It makes more sense for the teacher to be perceived as the friend, ally, and supporter who helps the student pass evaluations performed by someone else. So we recommend the alternative path evaluation panel. In some cases the panel will do the actual evaluating. The panel would include, for instance, a speaker of French who would interview the student who has studied French independently, or the student might show the panel a video tape which he or she has made. In other cases the panel would review the results of others' evaluations, such as objective test results or reports of supervisors. But in all cases the panel acts as an objective and external team which makes some final assessment of total competency.

2. The alternative learning counselor will also deal with problems. Even if the student has worked out a good evaluation system, he or she will still need the continuing support and advice of a skilled counselor. The counselor can help the student work out a contract which he or she can reasonably fulfill. The counselor can assist the student in developing an evaluation proposal which will be effective. The counselor can be instrumental in assisting the student in finding the appropriate resources. All these tasks assume importance at the beginning of the alternative path, where many mistakes will be made. But the counselor will also provide continuing support throughout the duration of the alternative path. Through periodic conferences, telephone conversations, and short personal letters, the counselor can provide the student with the emotional support to continue the program.

Given the importance of the counselor's role, it is essential that he or she be provided with sufficient time to do the job satisfactorily. If the counseling of students on alternative paths simply becomes one more additional assignment, the counselor will be inclined to make the alternative path learner a low priority. The alternative path learner is not a very visible individual who is likely to wait around the counselor's office until his or her presence becomes a nuisance. It will be too easy for the counselor to forget the student on the alternative path and then blame him or her for "lack of motivation." However, if time is provided for alternative path counseling, we can legitimately expect some form of accountability. How can time be provided? A later chapter suggests a restructuring of the counseling staff which will facilitate alternative path counseling without additional expense. If a school system does not wish to pursue that option, the counselor can be provided with time for alternative path counseling through a proportionate reduction in his or her regular student load.

3. The peer support group is also essential in solving problems. This group can be formed in the following way. First, the counselor identifies a group of six to ten students who are all traveling on alternative paths. To provide for maximum effectiveness, the students in the same group should be similar in age, although some diversity in background and aspirations would be beneficial. The counselor then locates a mature adult skilled in working with groups. The adult should be a volunteer interested in alternative path learning; he or she might be a retired teacher or other professional, a member of the clergy, a worker or housewife free in the evening who wants to keep professional skills polished. The adult acts as a convener and facilitator for the peer support group.

Together the group members decide where and when they will meet. At the outset weekly or meetings every two weeks are recommended, until the group has become cohesive enough to function effectively with fewer meetings. At the informal meetings students share briefly the results of their learning. They talk over common problems encountered. They help each other with learning difficulties. They turn up new resources for each other. And from time to time they hold some kind of social activity, which binds them even closer.

Through such a group, the alternative path student feels that he or she has a home. There is no longer a sense of isolation. The group is able to help an individual member over a low point, encourage a poorly motivated student to stay in the program, and provide positive feedback to those who are making progress.

With an effective evaluation system, a skilled and interested counselor, and a supportive peer group, the alternative path student will find nontraditional study an exciting and enriching experience. So we don't have to change the institution radically. We can help young people find their way around them.

References

Bailey, Stephen K., Francis V. Macy, and Donn F. Vickers. *Alternative Paths for the High School Diploma*. Reston, Virginia: National Association of Secondary School Principals, 1973.

Directory of Independent Study Programs. Educational Consultants, Inc., St. Louis, Missouri.

Gartner, Alan, Mary Kohler, and Frank Riessman. *Children Teach Children*. New York: Harper and Row, 1971.

Glatthorn, Allan A., and Jon Briskin. "School on Wheels," *Today's Education*, Vol. 62, No. 5 (May 1973), pp. 44–46.

Guide to Independent Study Through Correspondence Instruction. Washington, D.C.: National University Extension Association., n.d.

Levin, Henry. *The Costs to the Nation of Inadequate Education*. A Report to the Senate Select Committee on Equal Educational Opportunity. Washington, D.C.: Government Printing Office, May 1972.

National School Public Relations Asssociation. *Drop-outs: Prevention and Rehabilitation*. Washington, D.C.: NSPRA, 1972.

CHAPTER FIVE

New Approaches to the Curriculum

The alternative schools and alternative programs described in the preceding chapters should offer students a range of curricular options. How such choices can be provided in both alternative and conventional schools will be the thrust of this chapter. The chapter reviews the major curricular changes taking place in alternative schools, assesses their strengths and weaknesses, and proposes some alternative arrangements for giving students a choice of curricular structures.

Alternative schools, of course, are not the first to experiment with major curricular change. For years now, curriculum theorists have been arguing the merits of subject-centered versus integrated learning, of teacher-planned versus student-selected experiences. (See, for example, Chase, 1966.) But alternative school experimentation has given these questions a new relevance and immediacy.

New Goals

What are the goals of these alternative schools? Any systematic curriculum plan probably begins with a statement of goals, and even alternative schools have impressive goal statements. Almost all make mention of the basic skills. Beyond that there is a healthy diversity. The Arlington Satellite Junior High Schools in Massachusetts, for example, include "reduce the level of interpersonal conflicts" (Walker, 1973, p. 20). A description of the Agora of Berkeley, California, reports, "Ethnic awareness and multi-cultural awareness are the principal objectives of the school" (Walker, 1973, p. 22). Pasadena Alternative School in California is among many which include "learning to learn." The school's program description explicates this goal further as: "to provide students with a critical awareness of the learning process, a tolerance for ambiguity, a chance to make independent decisions about learning, and an opportunity to develop all aspects of their . . . make-up" (Walker, 1973, p. 6). The Community School in West Hartford, Connecticut, has three "generation gap" goals: "to learn about people and jobs through interaction and involvement in the world; to give insight into that mechanism called 'community' and the interdependence of the individual and the society in which he lives; to help students shed suburban isolation through experiences in the Hartford area" (Walker, 1973, p. 34).

How useful are such goal statements? The answer to that is unclear. On the one hand, most such statements seem like an afterthought, an attempt to add educational rhetoric to a program conceived on an ad hoc basis. There seems to be little evidence in most alternative school bulletins of an attempt to link course offerings to school goals.

On the other hand, there are those who argue that the goal-setting process is an essential part of alternative schools' curriculum planning. In fact, Mario D. Fantini argues that all alternative schools and alternative programs in the public sector should have common objectives:

> Another ground rule is that each school must be working toward the *comprehensive set of educational objectives* [italics in original]. . . . These objectives or educational goals must be common to all schools within the system of choice. They should include mastery of the basic skills: reading, writing, English, and sciences; nurturing of physical and emotional development; vocational and avocational preparation [Fantini, 1973, p. 42].

The author is not sure what "basic skills . . . English, and sciences" means and should like to find out more about "avocational preparation." However, it does make sense for a district planning an alternative school curriculum to begin with some understanding of the basic goals. The author finds Stephen Bailey, Francis Macy, and Donn Vickers' statement of their "minimum capacities" for the high school diploma much more useful:

> *Basic Skills.* Achievement of a minimum level of reading and computation skills . . . ability to communicate effectively, in writing or through some combination of writing and other visual media . . . or through speech or some other aural medium. . . . *General Knowledge.* Knowledge in several fields of learning. . . . Some judicious admixture of the following fields is essential: language, math, science, social science, and the humanities. An individualized program of study must be made appropriate both in nature and in content . . . to a student's goals, interests, and capacities. . . . *Social and Political Skills.* Knowledge of the individual and social consequences of personal and group behavior, including the knowledge of how individuals and groups relate to political institutions and processes in the American system. . . . *Personal and Career Planning Skills.* Ability to identify alternative futures—both in occupational and personal terms—and to select among these [Bailey, Macy, and Vickers, 1973, pp. 34–37].

With some agreement about essential goals, the staff can then add those idiosyncratic goals that will give each program its special uniqueness.

New Approaches to Independent Study

During the past ten years many conventional schools have experimented with various types of independent study plans, most of which have enabled the student to work independently in a resource center. The Abington North Campus in Pennsylvania has used such approaches since 1964; other similar programs have been extensively reported in the literature. (See, for example, Beggs and Buffie, 1965.) Such programs, however, have granted the student very limited autonomy. Typically, the student is able to control only the time and place of learning; the teachers control all other elements.

Now several alternative schools are giving the student almost total autonomy in fashioning independent study plans. In such extensive independent study, the student determines what area he or she wants to study, identifies the resources needed, works independently outside the school setting, and reports occasionally to a teacher on his or her progress. For example, in the Shaker Heights (Ohio) Catalyst Program, a student interested in a special independent study project checks with an adviser. The adviser helps the student find a sponsor, usually someone outside the school, for the project. The sponsor provides the student with some suggested readings and helps him or her find some type of experience-based independent project. The student fills out a "contractual agreement," which specifies the number of credits expected, the nature of the project, what the student will do to complete the contract, how the student wants to be evaluated, and what the student expects to learn. Such an approach gives the student total control over all aspects of learning; the school in this case controls only the credit requirement. One credit requires forty hours with a sponsor and eighty hours of independent study.

How do such extensive independent study projects seem to work? They seem to provide the highest degree of freedom; it is logically assumed, and strongly argued, that such programs of total independence give the student real experience in making decisions and in assuming responsibility for learning. Many alternative school people feel, however, that such total independence is appropriate only for the most mature students; less mature students flounder in the absence of teacher direction. These alternative school people also express concern that too much independence, when it takes the student out of the school for extended periods of time, results in too much isolation from peers.

Unstructured Learning

Some free schools explicitly reject all curricula structure. Learners and teachers assemble and simply respond to perceived
problems and passing interests. Harold Bennett, for example,
advises people planning a free school in this manner: "Don't
plan a curriculum. When you sit down and work out a plan for
what's going to happen, your ego gets involved. Then when the
kids don't follow the plan, you get frustrated and angry with
them. And learning becomes a drag. Instead of planning a curriculum, set your energy toward creating a relaxed environment" (Bennett, 1972, p. 37).

Such an approach is different from extended independent
study in that it typically focuses on a group, not an individual,
project, and involves the teacher as an initiator or catalyst.

In such an approach, which is a kind of design-of-no-
design, a teacher and a group of students assemble at a given
time each day and decide what new project or problem strikes
their fancy. Curriculum planning—if it can be called that—is a
matter of finding a new project: "let's build a dome," "let's
make a film," "let's visit some alternative schools." Typically,
in such unstructured programs, there are no constraints of
periods, classes, subjects, or even instructional roles. One of the
most honest descriptions of unstructured learning can be found
in James Herndon's *How to Survive in Your Own Native Land*.

Such total openness is attractive. It offers ultimate flexibility. It often generates spontaneous student interest. It
capitalizes upon the strengths of active learning. And it results
in a cooperative learning effort that at its best gets everyone
involved in supportive relationships.

But it has its problems. Student enthusiasm quickly dissi-
pates, and a curriculum built upon such ephemeral stuff just
doesn't have long-term impact. Some important kinds of learning are neglected because they don't happen to fit in with the
"let's build a dome" approach. You can't learn much about
chemistry or poetry or French by building domes. And the
program's very lack of structure means that the learner who

needs some greater sense of regularity and predictability begins to flounder, gets very anxious, and often drops out from sheer bewilderment and frustration.

Open Classroom

The term "open classroom" is used to describe an approach to learning which is somewhat more structured than that described as "unstructured learning." Although the term "open education," or "open classroom," is variously interpreted, it is used here to describe programs at the elementary and secondary level where the teachers have built in a subtle degree of structure. Typically, certain curriculum outcomes have been predetermined and resource centers have been provided. The learner is then free to explore independently, motivated by developing interests and available materials. Content is not organized by "subject" or sequenced by grade level. Most open programs also make use of multi-age grouping and cross-age tutoring. (One of the best explications of the theory and assumptions of the open classroom can be found in Barth, 1972.)

Although varying degrees of openness are being explored in thousands of elementary classrooms, fewer secondary schools seem to be adopting the idea *in toto*, since the subject-organized curriculum seems to militate against "orthodox" openness. However, the St. Paul Open School in Minnesota builds its program around the open classroom concept. The school includes children and young people of all ages. Each student selects an adviser from the staff. The adviser meets with the student weekly to help the student write goals and devise a program. The school's space is organized into several major resource areas called theaters of learning. The shop area, for example, enables students to work on their own projects in a variety of media—wood, metal, plastics, electronics, printing, duplicating, motors, welding, and so on. St. Paul supplements its theater-of-learning concept with several scheduled classes, some of which are available to students of all ages, others of which are restricted to certain age groups.

To many, the open classroom approach seems to combine the right mix of freedom and structure. But it has not been without its problems. St. Paul's is candid in its discussions of the problems its teachers faced:

> Teachers suddenly had to cope with the tough problems of student accountability, scheduling, responsible freedom, control and direction, how to intervene, providing stimulating choices, and messiness. Their thinking was yanked to and fro on concerns such as order and structure vs. disorder, the value of play, and how to develop self-discipline. Far from the appearance of being permissive and endorsing a lack of structure, teachers needed to learn great organizational and planning skills to reduce chaos and random wandering by children [Jennings, n.d., p. 6].

The Skills Exchange Curriculum

Traditionally, curriculum begins with some statement of goals, as explained earlier, and then specifies content to achieve those goals. One marked deviation from such a paradigm is the skills exchange curriculum, a curriculum idea brought into fashion through the alternative schools movement. In the "skills exchange curriculum," as the term is used here, the curriculum grows out of the skills of people who are available to teach. The skills and knowledges offered in such a curriculum typically have no orderly relationship with the goals of the school but are instead an idiosyncratic expression of the competencies of individuals.

One of the most extensive skills curricula is offered at Community Interaction Through Youth (CITY), a school-without-walls program operating in and serving students from the Cambridge–Brookline, Massachusetts, district. (The program also includes handicapped students from the Industrial School for Crippled Children.) During the second term of 1973–1974, for example, CITY made more than fifty courses available to its students in sites throughout the community. The following titles are typical of the broad range of offerings in the CITY program:

    Silk-screening
    Rembrandt Revisited
    Introduction to Cosmetology
    Radio Broadcasting
    Cooking with Natural Foods
    Introductory Guitar
    People to People About Fish
    Practical Law
    Hatha Yoga
    Scuba Instruction

The program identifies the academic area in which each course can be credited, the number of class hours a week each course will meet, and the number of credits that can be earned in each course.

A particular list of course offerings is determined solely by the community-based instructional sites where they are offered and the community people available to teach or serve as a "learning coordinator" on a volunteer basis. Thus, the project's curriculum development is described in the following way: "Curriculum development procedures, as they relate to the CITY program or project, call for the identification of suitable community-based instructional sites in conjunction with the identification of an on-site Learning Coordinator who will teach an alternative curriculum" (Cheatham, n.d., p. 4).

This community-centered skills exchange curriculum does not constitute the student's entire program at CITY. Each student must participate in at least two courses in the local high school. Many alternative schools supplement a basic curriculum with a skills exchange component, frequently drawing upon the competencies of teachers, parents, and students, as well as community volunteers.

The advantages of the skills exchange curriculum are several. First, there is an obvious fit between the curriculum and the instructional staff; the people teaching the courses are doing so because they have competencies in the areas being taught. Second, the curriculum is as varied and diverse as the talents of those recruited to do the teaching. Third, the curriculum is very flexible and can respond quickly to students' needs and interests. If a student wants to learn motorcycle repair, the school finds someone with that competency. Fourth, the skills exchange curriculum affords the use of competent youth and adults as teachers who are not certificated and who present to their students a role model different from that of the conventional teachers. Finally, since the instructional staff is often composed of volunteers, the program is also an effective way of decreasing total instructional costs.

The chief drawback to the skills exchange curriculum is its lack of order and system. There is no assurance that the skills exchange curriculum will provide a complete program for the student; the CITY offerings for the second semester in 1973–1974, for example, included no mathematics, chemistry, biology, or physics, and no course that seemed to provide an in-depth study of literature. The CITY sponsors have wisely handled this difficulty by requiring the student to take two of the courses at the home high school.

The Structured Subject Curriculum in the Alternative Setting

A structured subject curriculum in an alternative setting would include programs which are essentially like those of the conventional school. Courses are offered in the standard disciplines (English, science, social studies, etc.), with little attempt to integrate the disciplines. All courses run for the entire year, typically meeting daily in groups of 25–35. Extensive use is made of teacher-directed inquiry, with the teacher playing an active role in explicating the structure of the discipline.

While such an approach is often attacked as "traditional," it does have some obvious strengths, if we can put aside our biases against conventional designs. First, its high degree of structure seems to facilitate learning for many students who require stability, predictability, and familiarity. Second, the centrality of the teacher's role seems to make it effective for highly structured disciplines, like the advanced sciences, where too much openness and freedom are counter-productive. Finally, its very conventionality and familiarity free the faculty to deal with issues of school governance and climate, which some alternative educators see as more central than curriculum design.

But the problems of the approach are also clear enough. Its familiarity takes away some of the excitement of the alternative school setting; students complain that they are learning "the same old stuff." The heavy stress placed upon teacher direction often results in student passivity. The year-long courses militate against curricular flexibility. And the standard disciplines simply can't deal effectively with many critical problems that transcend their boundaries.

However, a few alternative schools have been able to use the structured subject curriculum as a vehicle for new content. The Urban Career Education Center in Philadelphia, for example, uses standard subject titles such as English, social studies, mathematics, and science. However, in addition to stressing the basic academic component of these disciplines, each course also includes content on self, community, and careers. Also, all courses have been developed in learning package form to facilitate self-paced learning.

Another career-oriented school also uses standard subjects as the vehicle for a career component. The High School for Health Professions in Houston offers standard academic subjects. However, health professions content is integrated with the academic component. A brochure from the Houston district explains the integration in this fashion:

> The regular academic courses such as biology, mathematics, English and foreign language are taught in the conventional manner—except the courses are being integrated with health concepts. In English, in addition to the regular classroom work, students must learn medical terminology and are given the opportunity to write essays and

themes on medical concepts and personalities. In foreign language students are taught to converse medically with patients in French or Spanish. Many concepts are taught in mathematics such as charting and medical statistics   ["High School for the Health Professions," n.d., p. 4].

The Mini-Course Curriculum

In general, when alternative schools depart from the conventional program, they move toward a random collection of short-term, focused mini-courses. Such an array of discrete offerings seems like a smorgasbord from which students pick and choose without concern for sequence or system. Such programs are almost always composed of courses lasting seven to twelve weeks, focusing on some limited problem or inquiry area. Typically, the course offerings are suggested by the teachers, although many alternative schools make a systematic attempt to get student input. Thus, an alternative school with a mini-course curriculum would offer an array of courses something like the following:

> The Jazz Age
> Macrame
> The Politics of Hunger
> French Cooking
> Motorcycle Repair
> Sexism in America
> Writing Poetry
> Zen and the Western World
> Improve Your Reading Speed

The advantages of such a curriculum design are clear. Its simplicity is attractive: there is no need for elaborate planning or systematic analysis; just get people together and let them offer whatever courses they want. It offers great flexibility; courses can be dropped or added with ease. And it is an effective way to get teacher and student input into curriculum: anyone interested is able to develop his own course without too much concern for theoretical questions of design and articulation.

But there are some obvious drawbacks. Such an approach results in a fragmented curriculum in which the total program seems to be just an unsystematic collection of bits and pieces. The student has little chance to make connections. Also, the absence of any plan or design often results in both duplication and omission. Thus, a school might readily offer four courses in women's studies but no course in basic reading skills. It's more exciting to plan and teach a course in "Women in Twentieth-Century America" than one in "Learning to Read." Finally, the "do your own thing" curriculum too often results in a frothy curriculum; too many of the courses are trivial in content and shallow in substance.

A group of conferees representing alternative schools expressed this concern about the smörgasbord curriculum: "There was also general agreement about the need to look very critically at the smorgasbord curriculum, and to begin this inquiry by recognizing that the mere consumption of educational courses from an expanded menu falls far short of our ultimate goals for alternative learning programs" ("Decision Making in Alternative Secondary Schools," 1972, p. 45).

This sort of dissatisfaction with the mini-course or smorgasbord curriculum has led alternative schools to supplement such a curriculum with other models, as shall be noted later.

The Core Curriculum

Borrowing curriculum ideas from the Progressive movement of the thirties and staffing notions from the team-teaching plans of the sixties, many alternative schools build their programs around a team of teachers working with a group of students in a block of time each day, studying some broad problem area. And some schools using such programs have even dusted off an old term from the later Progressive era, calling such programs their core courses. In a typical core or "broad fields" program, a teaching team composed of an English teacher, a social studies teacher, and a science teacher meet with a large group of students for two hours each day. For the first six weeks, they explore the concept "The Meaning of Community," examining the idea from literary, sociological, and biological perspectives. The next six weeks they might move to a unit on "Violence and Aggression," again examining the question from the perspective of the different disciplines.

Such core courses are often developed by teachers at alternative schools who are concerned about the fragmentation of the mini-course or smorgasbord curriculum. The staff at Metro in Chicago, for example, saw the core course as a way of integrating learning. A report on Metro describes the core course proposal as follows:

> The conception of the core course developed by the teams of three to four teachers who were working on the five core courses was that students would have individual projects or placements related to the central theme of the course, and then would meet in larger groups to relate their individual experience to the central theme. Thus, students in "Neighborhood Studies" worked with community organizations, tutored, made films, and interviewed people on the street in different neighborhoods. Then, they met in seminars to discuss similarities and differences between different neighborhoods in the city ["The Chicago Public High School for Metropolitan Studies," 1971, p. 13].

Such a design has much to offer. It facilitates—even mandates—staff cooperation. It provides for the utmost flexibility of time in its use of the block schedule. It provides a convenient vehicle for the use of community resources. And it shows the student that most of the important problems really cannot be compartmentalized into the artificial structures of the conventional disciplines. The student is able to make important connections quite readily and synthesize new ideas with much less difficulty than in the discipline-oriented curriculum.

But again there are problems. First, students with short attention spans complain about the dullness of long blocks of time and the boredom of having the same teachers. Second, the broad core program seems to take over and begins to crowd out subjects and teachers who can't fit into the grand design. Finally, although teachers talk sincerely about "integrating the basic skills," too often such skills are neglected in the concern for the big issues of Life and Death and Love and Faith.

After weighing such advantages and disadvantages, the staff at Metro concluded with this recommendation:

> There is a definite need for interdisciplinary learning experiences in the program, but these should grow more naturally out of cooperation between several teachers who want to work together, rather than being instituted across the board by a policy decision. . . . Participation in the course should have been limited to students who were strongly interested in one of the areas in which placement had already been set up or who had a very definite idea about the type of placement or project they were interested in ["The Chicago Public High School for Metropolitan Studies," 1971, p. 15].

Individualized "Packaged" Learning

Some alternative schools and a few of the more innovative conventional schools are attempting to individualize student learning through the extensive use of "learning packages." In such an approach, the student is placed in a subject at his or her own level of achievement, learns at his or her own pace, and does not move ahead until he or she has achieved mastery of the essential learning. Central to such programs are the learning packages, either teacher-made or commercially prepared, which are designed to facilitate self-instruction. While the specific features of the learning packages differ, almost all include a pretest, a statement of the learning objectives, suggested learning activities, self-assessment measures, and a final evaluation. In schools making extensive use of learning packages, the students work on their own in a learning resource center, with an aide providing any needed assistance. They schedule themselves to see the teacher once or twice a week for small-group activities and perhaps once a week for some kind of large-group session. In schools where more sophisticated technology is available, the individualized instruction is delivered through a computer terminal, but the basic model is still the same.

Teachers at Archbishop Ryan High School in Omaha, Nebraska, have written their entire curriculum in Learning Activity Packages, or LAPS, as they call them. Virginia Roth describes their approach to curriculum in this fashion:

This kind of package of work we call a Learning Activities Package (LAP). No one teacher at Ryan can disseminate a LAP until all the members of the department have critiqued it and concurred with it. This refines the work, keeps it sequential, and obviates unnecessary repetition. If a course has 24 objectives, we would describe three or four LAPS of six or eight objectives apiece in order to keep the learning hurdles low enough so that a student is not psychologically overwhelmed by the quantity of work [Roth, 1973, p. 16].

The Alternative Education Center in Grand Rapids, Michigan, uses programmed packages, along with a behavior modification system of external rewards to encourage the reluctant students to do the packages. One student was quoted as saying, "You know I hate it, but I do several of these learning packages every day" (Barr, 1974, p. 239).

Such an approach to individualization has much to recommend it. The students assume responsibility for their own learning. Under the best conditions, they develop important skills of learning how to learn. Also, the program in its essential design ensures that the student will be working at the appropriate level and achieving mastery at that level. Such an approach at its best would eliminate the scholastic failure caused by inadequate preparation. Also, such programs individualize the pace of learning, a key element in the learning process. Most students, if given enough time, can master the learning typically expected of secondary school students. Finally, under ideal conditions such programs enable the teacher to give more individual attention to students with problems.

But again there are real drawbacks which militate against the total success of such programs. To begin with, advocates assume that students are highly motivated to work on their own and do not require close teacher monitoring. The reality, of course, is otherwise. Many students are so bored and unmotivated that they will do as little as necessary to get by. Second, even motivated students, who begin to use the packages with enthusiasm, soon become bored with the daily routine of completing one learning package after the other.

Also, such an overemphasis on learning packages reduces the amount of student–teacher contact to below a desirable level. Students want to be able to work closely with a live teacher, not a collection of mimeographed pages. Finally, the packaged programs simply do not provide sufficient time for small-group learning and peer interaction. Students have strong social needs and do not want to spend too much time isolated in a study carrel.

Affective Learning

A growing number of alternative schools are making extensive use of affective curricula and learning experiences. In such programs the curriculum emphasizes feelings, processes, and values. In all areas of the school's program, efforts are made to relate the cognitive with the affective; for every concept developed, the teacher leads the student to examine how personal feelings and values relate to the topic at hand. And the learning processes make extensive use of small-group activities, with a heavy emphasis on such approaches as role playing, simulation, unstructured discussion, and improvisational drama.

One alternative school that has had much success with affective curricula is the School for Human Services in Philadelphia. Students in this school spend half a day in an affective classroom and half a day working in an institution for human services.

Affective programs are appealing in several ways. Their emphasis on feelings and values tends to personalize the learning and help the students find connections with their own experiences. The stress on small-group interaction is attractive to students and typically results in much student enthusiasm, at least initially. And the emphasis placed on active and creative learning makes a great deal of sense with a generation of passive youth.

But there are some difficulties, again. To begin with, for some of the significant academic learning in the school's curriculum, questions of personal feelings and values are simply irrelevant. Attempts to find issues of feelings and values in a subject like chemistry or algebra are rarely successful. Second, overemphasis on a single learning approach, even a very effective one, leads inevitably to student boredom. Eventually, the complaint is heard, "Do we have to do role playing again?" Finally, such programs often exclude or minimize learning strategies that emphasize teacher-directed inquiry and thus result in the neglect of an essential type of learning.

Lessons from Experimentation

What lessons can be drawn from this curriculum experimentation by alternative schools? There are several which are important.

First, the experimentation itself has been beneficial and productive. Even though the alternative schools have not found any single curricular answer to their instructional problems, they have opened up new territory, explored new approaches, developed new courses. And just the process of planning a new curriculum seems to produce a healthy excitement in the schools. All schools, therefore, can be safely urged to play with curriculum design; in the process they will make some exciting discoveries and generate student and teacher interest.

Second, students' interests shift rapidly and their enthusiasm for a given type of curriculum wanes quickly. No curriculum innovation will continue, by itself, to generate excitement for a long period of time; no given sequence of courses will always appeal to the ephemeral interests of teen-agers. These related conclusions suggest that at least part of the curriculum should be designed so that it can be changed easily, responding readily to new input from students and teachers.

Third, alternative schools and conventional schools can experiment freely with the "soft" curriculum—the relevant, the affective, the student-centered—as long as they provide for what both students and parents consider the basics. If the students are learning the basic skills and mastering the hard curriculum of mathematics and science, the school can safely play all the games it wishes with the rest of the curriculum. For this reason, most alternative schools experiment most boldly with the disciplines of the humanities.

Fourth, no single curriculum design can provide for all kinds of learning. Of all the approaches described, none seems to be a perfect model for all types of learning experiences. It seems to be difficult to learn calculus in anything except a calculus course.

In what ways can the alternative schools capitalize on the strengths of all approaches and give students an option about the curriculum? This is the concern of the following section.

Providing Curricular Options

Realizing that no single design for curriculum is ideal, alternative school people have tried three different approaches to offering options and capitalizing on the best of each. After describing each of these briefly, the author would like to propose a way of restructuring the secondary school curriculum.

One way to provide curricular options is to link a particular curriculum design with a specific kind of school environment. Chapter 3 showed one such model and explained how a given type of curriculum seemed to have a natural fit with a given environment. Thus, the unstructured curriculum fits best in the free school; the mini-courses and core curriculum in the alternative school; and so on. If such an approach is implemented too inflexibly, however, it denies the student the benefits of various approaches.

A second approach is to offer a given course in three different ways and then give the student a choice about the degree of structure. Thus, a student might be able to choose from among three different English courses described as follows:

1. Affective English. In this course you will learn to communicate more effectively by doing extensive work in groups. The main stress will be on your feelings and values, and the

learning activities will chiefly involve such active participation as role playing, simulations, games, fantasizing, and creating. If you want to find out more about yourself and like an experimental and experience-based approach, this course is for you.

2. Self-Instructional English. In this course you will be able to work at your own pace and use learning resources at your own level of achievement. Most of your work will involve the use of learning packages which will help you move as slowly as you need to or as fast as you wish. If you like to work on your own and to get immediate feedback about your learning, this course is for you.

3. Traditional English. In this course you will learn English through teacher presentation and class discussion. The course will stress the study of grammar, composition, and literature. If you learn best in a structured situation and enjoy class discussions and lectures, you will enjoy this course.

Such an approach gives the student honest information about how the course will be taught and gives him or her a choice about the way English is to be mastered. The Marshall-University High School in Minneapolis, Minnesota, offers the student three options for learning: the student may take traditional subjects, interdisciplinary studies, or independent directed study.

The third way of offering the student the benefits of the various approaches is to offer two or more of the models in the course of the school day. The Arlington (Massachusetts) Satellite Junior High Schools, for example, offer the following approaches to learning: basic skills laboratories, short-term mini-courses, big ideas courses, work and service experiences, skill exchanges, and informal classes.

And students in the Alternative Schools Project in Wyncote, Pennsylvania, spend part of the week in basic skills laboratories, part of the time in interdisciplinary core courses, part of the week in mini-courses, and one afternoon a week in open-ended independent study.

In all these ways students can have the advantages of several different approaches.

A Proposal for Comprehensive Restructuring

The curriculum experimentation in alternative schools indicates that both alternative and conventional schools can make the best provisions for learning by developing an overall curriculum design strategy that draws upon the strengths of all approaches. Such a recommendation is not advocated simply because of a mindless eclecticism but because each approach has something significant to contribute to the students' total learning.

The overall design strategy proposed would use each of the six basic approaches for those types of learning which could be optimally facilitated by such an approach. Before examining the specifics of such a design, let us present an overview of how the design might work. Table 6 identifies the curriculum approach, notes the types of learning which it seemingly facilitates best, and then gives examples of the subjects and courses which might be included in each approach.

With this basic framework in mind, let us look at each of the areas in greater detail, noting specific course offerings and possible organizational structures.

Structured Curriculum: Disciplined Knowing

Part of the school's offerings, the author believes, should be presented through the structured curriculum. He calls this phase the curriculum for disciplined knowing. This term is used to categorize all subjects in which the chief emphasis is on the structure of the discipline. In subjects like physics, calculus, linguistics, and economics, the Brunerian concept of "structure" becomes important, and questions of student interest and relevance secondary. The criteria to be used for including a course in this phase are:

1. The course constitutes a separate discipline and develops a unique way of seeing the world.
2. It constitutes an organized body of knowledge and is the object of scholarly study and investigation.

Table 6 Overview of Curriculum Design Strategy

Type of Curriculum Approach	Types of Learning Best Facilitated	Typical Courses
Structured Curriculum	Those subjects where continuity and articulation are important and a high degree of teacher direction is required	Foreign language, advanced science, and mathematics
Mini-course curriculum	Those courses focusing on specific problems or discrete skills	"Using Computers," "Media in Our Lives"
Broad fields	The study of larger questions and issues which require extended time and draw from several disciplines	"Building Community," "The Uses of Power"
Open-ended learning	Learning emerging from open-ended projects requiring minimal structure	Organic farming, dome building, film making
Individualized instruction	The development of specific learning skills where individual placement and pacing are critical	Learning to read, expository writing
Affective curriculum	Personal learning focusing on feelings and values	Personal growth seminar

3. It is abstract, theoretical, and symbolic, as opposed to concrete, practical, and literal.
4. Sequence and articulation are critical in understanding and mastering its essential concepts.

Using these criteria, the following subjects should be included in the area of disciplined knowing: biology, chemistry, physics, advanced mathematics, linguistics, economics, and foreign languages.

Other educators would, of course, have their own recommendations. Obviously, such divisions of the social sciences as anthropology, political science, sociology, psychology, geography, and history could be and are taught as disciplined knowing. The author's own preference, however, is to integrate these disciplines into other phases of the program.

The structured curriculum is clearly an ideal design model for maximizing learning in the area of disciplined knowing. Such organized disciplines are best learned through a highly structured curriculum. The following are recommended for this phase of the curriculum:

Schedule: meetings daily or three times a week, forty-to-sixty-minute periods, for entire year.
Group size: weekly large-group lecture; laboratory groups as required; two to three class-sized groups of 25–35 for teacher-directed inquiry; weekly small group for discussion.
Instructor: professional teacher plays highly active role in explicating structure and facilitating inquiry.
Source of curricula: national curriculum projects modified to suit local needs.
Basic teaching method: teacher-directed inquiry through lecture and guided discussion.

Clearly, then, the student should be told that part of his learning will take place in the structured curriculum, that in these areas there will be no "rap sessions," and that the teacher will not be especially interested in his feelings or opinions. In a sense, then, this constitutes the "hard" curriculum—and in each school there is a need for balance between the hard and the soft.

Mini-Course Curriculum: Survival Skills

Part of the school's curriculum should be presented through the mini-course curriculum. The author calls this phase the survival skills curriculum. This term is used to categorize all courses in which the chief emphasis is on developing some specific skill, knowledge, or competency required to survive in the contemporary world. In these courses all that counts is relevance. The course content should deal specifically with a societal problem or develop some personal competency. These are the criteria to be developed for including a course in this phase:

1. The course deals with some critical survival issue or problem.
2. It focuses on the applied, the practical, the present, the relevant.
3. It can be covered and mastered comfortably in a six-to-ten-week period with classes meeting a few hours a week.
4. It is a discrete course; sequence and articulation are of no consequence.

Using these criteria, the author proposes the following list of courses for consideration. Obviously, students and teachers should develop their own list; the list below is only for purposes of illustration. And the courses are grouped only to show the broad issues which may be considered germane to survival.

Ethnic studies
    Contemporary black literature
    Minorities in twentieth-century America
    Red man, white injustice
    The new ethnicity
Job and college
    College survival
    Planning your future

Getting and keeping a job
Note-taking skills
Improving your study skills
Information retrieval
Social issues
A woman's world
The law and you
Crime and criminal justice
Truth and television
Dealing with the bureaucracy
Environmental issues
Keeping the environment clean and green
Surviving in the city
Living cheaply
Life-styles and the environment
Architecture and the environment
Personal skills
Good drugs, bad drugs
You and your money
Making leisure count
Creative problem solving
Art of meditation
You are what you eat
Keeping physically fit
You and your sexuality
Aesthetic awareness
New art, old forms
The sounds of music
Contemporary design
You and your taste
The new journalism
Practical skills
Auto and cycle repair
Coping with the computer
Appliance repair
Typing
Baking and cooking
Home maintenance and repair

This list of course offerings should be sufficient evidence that the survival curriculum can best be accommodated in the mini-course format. The flexibility of this format and its openness to student input make it ideal for such offerings. The following features are important here:

Schedule: two to three times weekly, thirty-to-sixty-minute sessions, lasting for six to ten weeks.

Group size: small groups wherever possible.

Instructor: any competent person—professional teacher, student, volunteer.

Source of curricula: student- and teacher-developed.

Basic teaching method: small-group discussion, with limited instructor presentation.

Broad Fields: Integrated Studies

A third component of the school's program should be offered through the broad fields approach. The author calls this phase the integrated studies curriculum. This term is used for the in-depth study of fundamental questions of human concern that transcend the compartmentalized disciplines. The integrated studies curriculum is significantly distinct from offerings in the survival skills component; the survival skills courses are focused, practical, and timely; the integrated studies courses confront more general questions, are more theoretical and conceptual, and deal with timeless rather than timely issues. These are the criteria proposed for content in this area:

1. The courses confront general overarching questions that grow out of the human condition.
2. The answers to those questions draw from several disciplines and intellectual frameworks.
3. Wherever feasible, the course content draws from the perspectives of several cultures and world views.
4. The questions to be confronted have been important in the past, are critical now, and will probably be central in the future.

What issues meet these criteria and thus merit inclusion in this component of the curriculum? These are the topics proposed as being central:

The quest for self
The nature of truth
Making and finding beauty
Man and his gods
The meaning of love
The races of the world
The nature of goodness
The search for freedom
Building community
Power and violence

Clearly, these are the "big issues" that have always been the central concern of thinking man, and in some way the schools should help young people begin the process of finding answers. To do so will require time and effort; answers won't come through twice-a-week rap sessions.

The design principles of the broad fields approach are especially suited for dealing with questions of this magnitude. The longer blocks of time and the team-teaching arrangements are essential for significant study in this area. These then are the structures proposed for the integrated studies courses:

Schedule: two-to-three-hour sessions, two or three times a week, lasting for six to twelve weeks.

Group size: flexible, as teaching team sees need for large- and small-group discussions.

Instructor: professional teachers plus specialists, representing disciplines of science, English, and social studies.

Source of curricula: initial planning by teachers, with significant input from students.

Basic teaching method: independent study, small-group seminars, occasional lecture, extensive use of community resources.

Open-Ended Learning: Making and Working

The fourth component of the curriculum is presented through a completely open-ended structure which the author calls making and working. This term is used to describe that significant learning which comes about best through working at a job, doing volunteer service, traveling, and getting deeply involved in important creative projects. Each student would be expected to spend a significant amount of time during the course of the year working on his own in a real learning experience that transcends the concepts of "course" and "class." The learning that comes about through work, volunteer service, travel, and focused creativity may be the most important learning of all. Learning in this area would meet these criteria:

1. There is an absence of the artificial structures of courses, bells, and structured role relationships.
2. The learner is almost completely responsible for initiating his own learning, for pacing his own work, and for evaluating his own product.
3. Extended periods of time are required and long-term tasks are expected.

What specific kinds of making-and-working experiences are contemplated? These possibilities suggest themselves:

1. Working part-time for pay at a job of the student's own choosing; hopefully, the job will have some connection with long-range career plans.
2. Doing volunteer service in the student's own school, in a nearby elementary school, or in a variety of community agencies.
3. Undertaking some planned travel experience, with specified learning outcomes.
4. Completing some major independent study project which requires extensive research in field, laboratory, and library.
5. Completing some creative project—making a film, producing a play, composing music, building a dome, pub-

lishing a newspaper or magazine, constructing furniture, making a sculpture.

Such tasks obviously require the freedom from structure that is implicit in the open-ended learning design. The following should make clear the extent to which there is this freedom from structure:

Schedule: student has long blocks of time—extended hours in either the morning or the afternoon—for a week or several weeks in a row.

Group size: student works on his own or with a small group of fellow students.

Instructor: student may be working completely on his own or drawing from the expertise of any competent adult.

Source of curriculum: the job, the service, the travel, or the project itself; no formalized course.

Basic teaching method: apprenticeship, working, independent inquiry.

Individualized Instruction: Basic Learning Skills

An important part of the student's academic program will be presented in the individualized teaching mode in a phase called basic learning skills. This program area focuses on what used to be called the three Rs—reading, writing, and basic arithmetic. Despite all the technological advances, these old-fashioned skills still seem essential as the fundamental tools of learning and thus need continued emphasis.

Under this program area, then, only three course offerings may be proposed: basic reading skills, basic writing skills, and basic computational skills. The reading course would stress comprehension and word-attack skills; the writing course would focus exclusively on expository writing; and the computational skills course on the basic arithmetical processes. Higher-level skills in each of these areas would be covered in one of the other programs; the emphasis here is solely on the basic skill levels.

As each student enters the school, he would be given diagnostic tests to establish his level of achievement in these areas. Although standardized tests are not precise measures of accomplishment, they do give rough indications of achievement and can be used to help counselors and teachers place the student at the appropriate level in reading and basic mathematics. Teachers could develop their own simple composition test to measure writing achievement, or they could use one of the standard composition achievement tests.

The staff would use the results of these diagnostic measures in a conference with the student and the parent. Although the extent to which a given curriculum or program should be required will depend on the staff's philosophy about this matter, the following would be recommended:

If the student's test results indicate he is achieving two or more years below grade level in an area, he should be *required to take* the course.

If the student's test results indicate he is achieving at grade level or one year below grade level, he should be *advised to take* the course.

If the student's test results indicate he is achieving above grade level, he should be *advised to substitute* other courses.

All three courses should be totally individualized. The year begins with precise diagnosis of achievement. The student is placed at an appropriate level. He works at his own pace at that level until he achieves the necessary degree of mastery. As he progresses through the learning unit, he is given immediate feedback about his progress; if he is not achieving at a satisfactory level, he is provided with specific remediation.

The individualized learning mode is ideal for the accomplishment of these objectives. Its emphasis on diagnosis, prescription, feedback, mastery, and self-pacing provides an optimal climate for the development of these critical skills. These specific structures are recommended:

Schedule: student schedules himself into laboratory and is expected to complete a certain amount of work each week.

Group size: student works on his own or with another student.

Instructor: aide in charge of laboratory.

Source of curriculum: materials developed by teachers, national research laboratories, or major publishers.

Basic teaching method: programmed learning.

Affective Curriculum: The Personal Growth Seminar

The final aspect of the program is presented through the structures of affective learning. The author calls this aspect the personal growth seminar. His argument here is that each student should spend perhaps two to three hours a week with a counselor–teacher (whose role is described in Chapter 7) and a small group of peers in the personal growth seminar. The entire emphasis in this seminar is on dealing with the student as a person, on helping him find himself and make connections. All the learning experiences should therefore meet these criteria:

1. They should relate directly and immediately to the student's personal life and to his or her relationships with others.
2. They should be concerned primarily with affective learning.
3. They should require the student's active participation through role playing, gaming, improvisation, and discussion.

The personal growth seminar does not deal with units of study, but is based upon dynamic learning experiences that confront these questions:

1. What am I like?
2. What are my strengths and talents?
3. What are my talent weaknesses?
4. How do others see me?
5. How can I learn to express my feelings more openly?
6. How can I develop the skills of relating openly with other people?
7. How do I function as a group member?

8. How can I become actively involved in the governance of the school?

9. What school problems do I have and how can I deal with them more effectively?

10. What personal and family problems do I choose to share with others and how might I cope with them more effectively?

11. What is the nature of my present value system and how can I make value decisions?

Other questions, of course, will be generated as the group becomes cohesive and develops its own agenda. The above are merely suggested as some of the possibilities that the group might want to consider. Such questions can best be answered through the mode of affective learning, where the emphasis on group processes seems ideally related to the goals.

The following is how to perceive the structure of this component of the program:

Schedule: two hours weekly, all year.

Group size: eight to twelve.

Instructor: teacher–counselor.

Source of curriculum: structured group exercises as developed by staff or adapted from published materials.

Basic teaching method: affective strategies—role playing, discussion, gaming, improvisation.

Such a comprehensive revision of the curriculum will clearly present a major challenge to the faculty. And obviously much more work needs to be done here in terms of implementation strategies and organizational specifics. However, the design in its present form does have these advantages:

First, it draws upon the strengths of several different approaches to the curriculum. Rather than arguing for a single model or design, it says in effect that each approach has its own unique strengths that can be integrated into a total program.

Second, it provides a dynamic balance between freedom and discipline, structure and openness. And the amount of structure is not determined simply by caprice or ideological bias but by a rational attempt to fit the structure to the nature of the learning goal.

Third, it offers the student a program that encompasses a variety of teaching approaches and learning styles. There is much less likelihood that the student will become bored.

Fourth, it gives explicit attention to the major skills required for learning in school and functioning in society. Important learning outcomes are not left to chance or vaguely "integrated."

Finally, it provides a vehicle through which conventional schools can draw upon and learn from the success and failure of alternative school curricula.

Therefore the design deserves careful consideration, but it is not the intent here to develop one more ideal model and impose it on teachers and administrators. Rather the concern has been to describe the new approaches being used by alternative schools and then to illustrate how all these approaches might be integrated into a new curriculum design.

But each school needs to develop its own design strategy. The author simply feels very strongly that the most effective school program will be one that draws upon the strengths of these several approaches, provides the student with a variety of learning experiences and teaching styles, and makes a better fit between learning goals and curriculum structure.

References

Bailey, Stephen K., Francis V. Macy, and Donn F. Vickers. *Alternative Paths to the High School Diploma.* Syracuse, New York: The Policy Institute of the Syracuse University Research Corporation, 1973.

Barr, Robert D. "Diversifying the Social Studies: The Trend Toward Optional Public Schools," *Social Education,* Vol. 38, No. 3 (March 1974), pp. 237–242.

Barth, Roland S. *Open Education and the American School.* New York: Agathon Press, 1972

Beggs, David W., and Edward G. Buffie. *Independent Study.* Bloomington: Indiana University Press, 1965.

Bennett, Harold Z. *No More Public Schools*. New York: Random House, 1972.

Chase, Francis S. "School Change in Perspective," in *The Changing American School*, edited by John I. Goodlad, Sixty-fifth Yearbook, National Society for Study of Education. Chicago: University of Chicago Press, 1966. Part 2, pp. 271–306.

Cheatham, Alflorence. *C.I.T.Y.: An Idea in Reality*. Cambridge, Massachusetts: Cambridge Public Schools, n.d.

"Chicago Public High School for Metropolitan Studies, The," Chicago: Urban Research Corporation, 1971.

"Decision Making in Alternative Secondary Schools," Chicago: Center for New Schools, 1972.

Fantini, Mario D. *Public Schools of Choice*. New York: Simon and Schuster, 1973.

Herndon, James. *How to Survive in Your Native Land*. New York: Simon and Schuster, 1971.

"High School for the Health Professions," Houston, Texas: Houston Independent School District, n.d.

Jennings, Wayne. "St. Paul Open School: Design, Rationale, and Implementation," St. Paul, Minnesota: Saint Paul Public Schools, n.d.

Roth, Virginia. "A Model for an Alternative High School." Austin, Texas: Austin Writers Group, 1973.

Walker, Penelope. *Public Alternative Schools: A Look at the Options*. Amherst, Massachusetts: National Alternative Schools Program, 1973.

CHAPTER SIX

Community-Based Learning

The previous chapter stressed the need for several types of community learning as a central part of the school curriculum. This chapter provides a rationale for such use, describes the forms it can take, discusses ways of relating it to the curriculum, and suggests some practical implementation strategies.

A Rationale for Community-Based Learning

For decades past, the school and community have existed in an uneasy and unhealthy relationship. They were seen as two separate worlds, with the wall between them breached only periodically by sporadic attempts at "community involvement." Consequently, they often perceived each other as adversaries, competing for dollars, space, and children's loyalties.

The students suffered most from this unhealthy relationship. They were buffeted between two worlds, often with two quite different standards. They were torn by two conflicting sets of demands upon their time and allegiance. And they were most critically deprived by being shut off from the real learning that can take place only outside the artificial world of the school.

Alternative schools have taken the lead in showing us that a new kind of relationship is possible and that the community can and must become the most exciting classroom of all. And, as indicated in the discussion of open-ended learning in Chapter 5, all schools should provide time for action learning in the community. Now the scholars have caught up with alternative schools practice; the report by James Coleman and his colleagues on youth recommends extensive involvement in work and service (Coleman et al., 1974).

For several reasons extensive use of the community for learning makes eminent good sense. First, community-based learning, when conducted with sensible safeguards, is an excellent way of strengthening school–community relationships. Students seriously engaged in learning make excellent ambassadors of goodwill. Second, community-centered learning reduces in-school pressures. Students who have a chance to move out into the community are better able to tolerate the more restrictive atmosphere of the school when they have to be there. The community can also provide resources in people and places that no school can provide. But most important, community-based learning is real learning that makes more impact, carries greater weight, and provides deeper insights than the artificial learning of the classroom.

This is not to say that community-based learning is without its drawbacks. It presents serious administrative problems of transportation, supervision, accountability, and safety. Second, integrating such learning with the ongoing life of the school is difficult, so that teachers who stay behind to teach classes often perceive extensive community-centered learning as disruptive. Finally, skillful teaching is required to integrate the community-based learning with the academic and to help the student make some sense out of his raw experience. Too many teachers erroneously believe that as long as the student is outside in the community doing something, he is having a significant learning experience. He well may be, but he would be learning even more if a skillful teacher were helping him integrate the community learning into his total educational growth.

Despite these drawbacks, however, community-centered learning does make sense, as the experience of numerous alternative schools will testify. The forms it can take are many and varied.

Some Types of Community-Based Learning

Travel

For years now schools have given uneasy approval to student travel. It was typically relegated to summer or holiday periods, or limited to the fun and games of a senior trip. But now a mobile generation is reminding us of some old lessons: that travel to other cultures and distant places can be truly educational, that the experience of traveling and living together can result in real growth, and that there is no substitute for real-life contact with people in other parts of the country or in other nations.

Alternative schools have taken the leadership in responding to these lessons by developing a variety of travel experiences. They have sponsored and conducted trips lasting from a few days to several months. Students have traveled by car, bus, boat, train, and airplane. The size of groups has ranged from four or five to an entire school of 150. And the trips have covered every part of this nation and major parts of Canada, Central America, Europe, and Asia.

Reports from the schools have extolled the virtues of such travel. Almost without exception the travel experience has been for students the highlight of the year, often serving as a means of pulling the school through a major crisis by rebuilding a sense of community. Not too surprisingly, perhaps, the students who traveled have reported that the major benefit they derived was in forming closer relationships with each other. in learning how to get along together in cramped quarters, in discovering new depths in peers whom they had known only superficially. They talk at length also about the practical skills they learned—of doing their own cooking, of working out their own schedules, of negotiating all the ordinary hurdles of police, customs officials, and other tourists. And they speak also of new insights and understandings derived about other cultures, other people, other ways of life.

The trips have not been without their problems, however; often the problems are quite serious. There are always a few accidents. People get lost. Adolescents continue to act like adolescents, perpetrating various kinds of foolishness that often reflect negatively on the school. And people in small towns abroad don't always welcome hordes of American teen-agers who swoop down on them, cameras and tape recorders in hand.

But such problems with school travel can be minimized if the teachers and students do some commonsense planning. The following steps can minimize the problems that do develop:

1. Take out adequate travel and liability insurance to be sure that all involved are fully covered.

2. Involve parents extensively in the planning of the trip, being sure that all are thoroughly briefed about the details.

3. Ensure that students take along schoolwork that can be done on the trip and provide time during each day when the work must be done.

4. Thoroughly orient students about the people and places they will be seeing. Make them especially sensitive to the mores of the people they will be visiting. Help them avoid the little mistakes that will mark them as "ugly Americans."

5. Have students and teachers develop together an explicit code of conduct for the trip—with appropriate penalties. The code should be simple and enforceable. One of the most effective the author has used contained only six words: no drugs, no alcohol, no sex. And any offense meant the person would be sent home at once.

6. Plan an itinerary that keeps everyone busy without their feeling rushed. Many travel problems develop because the adults planned itineraries that were crowded, with schedules that were too tight. Large groups of teen-agers can't keep tight

schedules; the anger and frustration that result from frequent lateness aren't worth the few extra minutes of sight-seeing.

7. Work out in advance some simple means of keeping people back home informed. When the travel is within the continental United States, a telephone chain is most effective: one student calls his parents and that parent begins the chain back home.

8. Spend part of each day while traveling in some kind of informal briefing sessions that help everyone involved make sense of what is happening. The briefing sessions should cover not just the travel experiences but the way people are fulfilling their responsibilities and getting along together.

9. Make the travel experience pay off educationally for others by providing ways for the students to share their experience with the rest of the school when they return. The exact form of the reporting—whether a special program in a community meeting, a slide-tape show, an exhibit, or informal discussions—should be left to the students.

Such commonsense measures can ensure that the travel component of the out-of-school learning has maximum yield with minimum trouble.

The forms that school travel take are numerous. The following list suggests just some of the possibilities:

1. French classes journey to French Canada.
2. Spanish classes visit Central America.
3. Art students tour museums and artist colonies.
4. Drama classes tour important theaters, performing as they go.
5. Social studies classes tour important historical places in America.
6. Students studying new life-styles visit open communes.
7. Science classes visit the Everglades and study it as an ecological community.
8. Students interested in architecture and city planning visit selected cities and new towns.

9. Music students visit New York for firsthand study of jazz and contemporary music.
10. Students plan and conduct a "survival trip," seeing how little they need for survival on an extended trip.
11. Under trained adult leadership, students participate in "encounter travel," where primary emphasis is placed on developing group skills and personal relationships.
12. Students embark upon a "service-travel" program, in which they journey to a disaster area and work there until their help is no longer needed.
13. School sponsors a "Faces of America" trip, during which students will take photographs and write poetry and prose about the people they meet, with the best results being published in a school magazine.
14. A "travel" course meets every weekend, with students responsible for planning each trip so that it has some kind of educational outcome.
15. School conducts a "Discover the South" journey, with students doing extensive reading before and during the trip, focusing on the old and new South.

Some trips will have a special focus, like those indicated above; others may be more open-ended, with the emphasis solely on the travel experience itself. All of it will be beneficial.

Work and Apprenticeships

Traditionally, schools have perceived work experience as a second-rate substitute for classroom learning. Usually it was offered to students who could not handle academic challenges. Consequently, the work experience provided through cooperative vocational and distributive education programs has been limited to the less able students not interested in a college education. The irony, of course, is that such students, typically from working-class families, were often those who least of all needed work experience. They were working; they knew the work ethic; they rubbed elbows with the gritty world of labor. And through such shortsightedness the schools denied the benefits of work experience to the affluent, middle-class youth who most of all needed the character development that only hard work can bring.

The young person who considers himself gifted because he is highly verbal needs the challenge of working with his hands. The self-centered adolescent who thinks his whims must always be satisfied should have the discipline of subordinating his momentary desires to the exigencies of holding a job. The spoiled teen-ager who has been given everything should know the excitement of earning and controlling his own money. The immature adolescent who thinks punctuality and good attendance are only teacher hang-ups has to learn how insensitive a demanding boss can be. The more affluent and soft our society becomes, the more adolescents need work experience. And the less their own lives bring them in touch with the world of work, the more the school should provide that experience for them.

It will not be easy, of course, for the schools to do so. Jobs for youth seem scarcer than ever before. (Note, however, that a survey by Havighurst, Graham, and Eberly, 1972, p. 18, indicated that there would be enough jobs for all youth between the ages of fifteen and twenty, if the jobs were limited to three hours a week.) Federal funding for work–study programs is understandably limited to the financially needy. Most companies are not altruistic enterprises with a mission to educate youth. Unions will resist any attempt which reduces the number of jobs available to their members. And middle-class parents may have some negative feelings about their son-to-be-a-doctor getting his hands dirty in a factory.

Such problems are not insurmountable, however. An aggressive campaign can be mounted to educate the parents and the general public. Parents who are working can help locate jobs in their own places of employment. A few civic-minded owners of small businesses can be prevailed upon to provide leadership in the business community. Union representatives can advise on procedures to avoid school–union conflicts. And pressure can be brought to bear upon the school district and the local township to practice what they preach and reserve part of their budget to hire students on work–study plans.

What form can work–study programs take? Several suggest themselves:

1. Apprenticeships. Individual students can apprentice themselves to professionals, craftsmen, and technicians. Pacific High School (Box 908, Montara, California) arranges through its Apprenticeship Service Program numerous apprenticeship positions throughout the nation.

2. Open-ended assignment to a single company. A student might have the most productive experience if he or she is assigned to a company that agrees to rotate him or her through a series of different work experiences. The Career Academy of Research for Better Schools in Philadelphia uses such an approach with good results.

3. Work in an area related to a career interest. Students interested in the health professions should have some experience working in unskilled jobs in hospitals just to give them a view of that world; students interested in teaching should work as clerks for teachers. While such jobs will of necessity be entry positions, they will provide some firsthand contact with that milieu.

4. Jobs designed to broaden the young person's occupational horizons. If an adolescent has fixed too soon on a career interest, the school can help him broaden his understanding of the world of work by arranging for him to work in an area totally unrelated to his stated area of interest. If a fifteen-year-old student thinks he or she wants to be a doctor, perhaps the best experience would be to work in a fabric store, where he or she might develop a latent talent in decorating.

Some schools, such as Manual High School in Denver arrange for work experience through specific courses with an explicit work-experience focus. Courses such as the following are offered by Manual and other high schools:

Legal Occupations Preparation
Orientation to Educational Professions
Health Services Occupations
Careers in Merchandising and Retailing
The Transportation Industry

Such courses could best be offered as short-term mini-courses, with the academic component limited to a seven- or nine-week period and the work experience running throughout a semester.

Since so many young people work during the summer when jobs are somewhat more plentiful, at least in the area of recreational services, it might be advisable for schools to develop simple procedures by which students could earn academic credit for appropriate types of work experience in the summer. A student working in a dining room at a mountain resort could do some special reading and study in food service occupations; a student working in a seashore hotel might undertake a special project in resort hotel management. In such cases the student finds a job and then uses that job as a focus for career study.

Other structures are, of course, possible. The important concern is how to help young people learn from meaningful work, not the advantages of a given structure.

Volunteer Service

In a time when paying jobs are in short supply, schools might give more serious consideration to providing volunteer service opportunities for young people. In fact, a few schools have experimented with a volunteer service requirement; to meet the requirement students are expected to contribute six hours of their time each week to some form of volunteer service.

Volunteer service has a few advantages over work experience from the school's point of view. First, it is easier to find nonpaying positions; the school need not spend so much time in locating hard-to-find paying jobs. Second, since the position is voluntary, the student and the school can play a more active role in defining the nature of the position, so that it has more educational benefits. Finally, volunteer service will appeal to many idealistic young people who are rejecting a materialistic life-style.

There are, however, some real problems with volunteer service. First, many agencies exploit their volunteers, giving them only the most menial and unrewarding tasks to do. Also, the volunteer is too often perceived as a person without status by the paid workers. Finally, the student is likely to regard the volunteer position with less seriousness than a paying job; he or she will be late or absent more often and will be more inclined to quit when minor frustrations develop.

Despite these drawbacks, however, alternative schools, and conventional schools as well, have found that volunteer jobs have a high payoff for the student. The student learns new job skills, develops good working habits, is introduced to new people and new ways of living, and feels psychologically rewarded by finding he or she is needed. This last point is worth stressing. In an affluent and technological society, youths are likely to feel unwanted and superfluous; such feelings intensify the periodic depression and anxiety they all know. The volunteer job can help them discover some meaning in their lives, some purpose in their days.

Opportunities for volunteer work abound in any community. And it seems preferable for a young person to serve in his own community, rather than feel he has a mission to "save" people in an alien community, who won't especially welcome his efforts at salvation. Hospitals, libraries, business offices, fire companies, animal hospitals, offices of local governments, local parks and playgrounds, nursery schools all need and welcome volunteer help.

Two opportunities for volunteer service should be mentioned specially. First, schools should take the leadership in helping young people find volunteer opportunities to serve old people. One of the tragedies of our culture is the way we isolate old people from the mainstream of our society, exacerbating the generation gap and making them feel like castoffs. The schools can provide needed leadership by enabling young people to volunteer in homes for the aged, in nursing homes, and in community agencies that work with the aged.

Second, young people should work in their own schools. It has been amply demonstrated that when young people tutor their peers, both the teacher and the taught benefit immeasurably. (See, for example, the numerous examples in the newsletter "Resources for Youth," National Commission on the Resources of Youth.) And at a time when classes are overcrowded, teachers increasingly busy, and students more in need of individual attention, some type of peer-tutoring and peer-counseling program seems essential. (A good description of how peer counseling can work can be found in Hebeisen's *Peer Program for Youth*, 1973.)

Informal Study in the Community

The community not only provides a rich resource for travel, work, and volunteer service; it also typically offers other types of organized learning experiences which schools should take advantage of. An important part of one's education does come about through organized learning in courses, but all such courses need not be taken in the public school.

The following list of offerings outside the public school only suggests the variety typically available in any metropolitan community:

Self-defense programs
Yoga instruction
Music lessons
College courses for auditing
Meditation workshops
Adult evening courses
Special seminars at libraries and museums
Language and culture courses at Hebrew or other religious schools
Courses and workshops conducted by local artists and craftsmen in art centers
Correspondence courses from colleges and universities
Television courses offered by colleges for credit
Lecture series on audio cassettes available commercially
Programs at neighborhood Y's and recreation centers

The problem typically is not finding available offerings, but in helping the young person choose out-of-school courses that will have sufficient substance and will relate to his educational goals. Too often the student is likely to take some trivial course that titillates him just for a few weeks; he then loses interest in it and drops it, having wasted his time and money.

Another problem concerns educational accountability. Later in this chapter some ways the school can systematize all the community-based learning experiences are suggested. Suffice it here to say that it is especially important to be sure that a student who wants credit for out-of-school courses gets them approved in advance, that the competency of the instructor is verified, and that the source of the programs is legitimate. The counter-culture has spawned a new breed of charlatans, who are offering courses in "psychic awareness" that sometimes turn out to be drug-baited traps for the innocent.

In addition to organized courses, young people should be encouraged to set up their own "skill exchange" or "learning network" inside or outside the school. In the skill exchange or learning network, people of all ages interested in teaching indicate to some central source the skills they have and the knowledge they are ready to share; people interested in learning write or call in to find out who is available. For example, if a computer programmer is interested in teaching programming and a young person is interested in learning programming, the network puts them in touch with each other.

Several networks have already been established in some of the metropolitan areas. Some charge a small fee; others are supported by foundation grants and other contributions. At the time this was written, one of the most active of such exchanges was Opening Networks (613 Winans Way, Baltimore, Maryland).

A learning network is a good project for high school students to organize themselves, either inside or outside the regular school. In simple operations a card file can be arranged by skills available; more complex networks can be programmed for computer retrieval. In all cases the basic principle is the same—putting people together who want to teach and learn.

Community As a Problem to Be Solved

For years Progressive educators have touted the value of the community as an object of study. Too often, however, such programs turned out to be somewhat superficial examinations of the local government, simple-minded surveys of local industries, or infantile field trips to zoos and museums. Teachers justifiably became cynical about playing such games, and the students themselves protested after the fifth visit to the local police station.

There is, however, a critical need for young people to study their own community in depth. This in-depth study would involve some systematic analysis of a single problem area, with the necessary background reading and the continuing assistance of a sensitive teacher, who can help the young person see the complexities and subtleties of modern problems.

Here are just a few of the questions that such a study could attempt to answer:

How does this community provide for its aged?

How does traffic flow affect business, industry, and living arrangements?

What key people really control the political power of the community?

What population shifts can be expected to take place in the next ten years?

How do zoning laws work to stratify the community?

How does the community deal with juvenile offenders?

Which industries are the biggest polluters? What economic problems would be involved in enforcing pollution laws?

What changes are taking place in family life-styles?

The author would stress again that such study can be meaningful only if it examines these questions in depth. The first question, for example, on the care of the aged should not simply be answered by a flying visit to one or two homes for the aged, but should require an in-depth study that makes use of several resources and critically looks at all sides of the question. Such a study might make extensive use of readings, films, seminar discussions, interviews with the aged, role playing, in-depth case studies, and extended visits to answer such related questions as the following:

How do other cultures provide for the aged?

How did our community provide for the aged fifty, one hundred years ago?

In what ways, do commentators predict, will this community care for its aged fifty years from now?

How much money do the state and local governments spend on care for the aged?

How are the aged treated in business places in the community?

What could be done to make a local nursing home a more attractive place for old people?

How adequate is the medical care for the aged?

Who provides for their spiritual needs?

What do the old people themselves want most of all?

These are only a few of the questions which could be asked by people who want to get beneath the surface of the question.

Some excellent suggestions for studying the community as a problem to be solved can be found in the book *Yellow Pages of Learning Resources* (Wurman, 1972). Its suggestions for study are applicable to any community, and the approach it takes could be readily adapted to any locality.

The Community As a Happening

The community can also be studied in more informal and unplanned ways which help the students to see it with a fresh eye. In this use of the community as a happening, the teacher and students might decide each day what they will look for and seek out as they walk through the crowded streets of the city or the shopping mall of the suburb. Such use of the community perhaps can be best facilitated through a regular course, where a creative teacher finds ways of linking class study with the life of the community. In contrast with the study of the community as a problem to be solved, the community as a happening emphasizes the unplanned, the unpredicted, the spontaneous and makes extensive use of on-the-spot observations.

Here are some of the possibilities that might develop when the community is seen as a happening:

Copy and analyze all the graffiti you find.

Photograph all the beautiful faces you see.

List all the ways that people in a housing development individualize the exteriors of their homes.

Analyze homeowners by categorizing their lawns and gardens.

Follow a young teen-ager in a shopping mall. Follow an old person. Contrast the paths they take and the places they stop.

Record the sounds of a city street, of a lake in the country, of a filling station in the suburbs.

Stand on a street corner and note all the odors you smell.

Make a recording of black youth "signifying" or "playing the dozens" (games of verbal abuse popular with urban black youth).

Observe children on a playground at recess time; note the games they play and the rhymes they chant.

Collect samples of as many different wild flowers as you can find on a country road.

Make a list of the models and years of automobiles in lower-class, middle-class, and upper-class neighborhoods. Draw whatever conclusions you can.

Contrast the advertisements found in cities and suburban shopping centers.

Make a list of the names people give their homes and estates in suburban and rural communities. What can you conclude about such people?

Make a list of the names that developers give to housing developments. Analyze the probable reasons for such choices.

Photograph the oldest buildings in town.

Make closeup photographs of a brick, the bark of a tree, a telephone pole, a doorbell.

As can be seen from the list, one of the major objectives of the community-as-a-happening explorations is to help young people develop skills of observing and understanding an environment they take for granted.

Implementation of Community-Based Learning

How can the school best provide systematically for such community-based learning experiences? As indicated before, such learning does require close supervision and monitoring if it is to be totally effective and not cause inordinate difficulties for the school. Several approaches are possible here.

First, some schools require community-based learning and make it a regular part of the student's program. At the School for Human Services in Philadelphia, the student spends half of each day in school-based study; most of the school's curriculum is affectively oriented, it so happens. And the student is required to spend the other half of the day working with some agency for human services—a hospital, school, nursing home, community agency, and the like. A similar requirement is in effect at the Career Academy sponsored by Research for Better Schools, also in Philadelphia. In this career school, supported by United States Office of Education funds for career education, a major part of the student's program is conducted in various offices and factories, where the student gets his career education firsthand.

In such programs, where the community-based learning occupies a major part of the school's offerings, the school typically has on its staff one or more individuals who are totally responsible for all community-based learning, lining up positions, arranging for interviews, monitoring success on the job, and smoothing out problems with employers. Also in such programs the student is usually given large blocks of what could be considered school time to do his work or volunteer service. Schedules for in-school learning are adjusted, so that the student is, for example, at school in the morning and on the job in the afternoon.

A second approach is to relate the community-based learning to a specific course or a related set of courses. In this course approach, only the students who register for the indicated courses are expected to undertake significant community involvement. Several alternative schools across the country are offering such courses, with titles like the following:

The Community as a Laboratory
Institutions—a Study of a Community
Community-Based Learning
Peer Teaching and Tutoring for Credit
Counseling for Teens
Traveling Seminar
Prisons, Parks, and Playgrounds—the Places in Our Town
Careers in Retailing and Merchandising

In this course approach, the teacher of the course usually becomes primarily responsible for the community-based learning, and must assume such responsibilities in addition to his regular teaching load. In many cases this means that the job is not too effectively performed, because the teacher often gives first priority to the classroom component.

Courses which stress community-based learning are given large blocks of time in the school's schedule to facilitate the use of the community. Alternative East in Elkins Park, Pennsylvania, for example, set aside a full day for its Institutions course, so that students were able to take extended field trips without interrupting other classes. Other schools provide large blocks of time in the afternoon for the same purpose. A few venturesome schools have offered community-centered courses in the evenings and have encouraged parents to enroll in them.

Third, some schools suspend classes for an extended period of time so that the entire school can become involved in community-based learning. In this pattern the school follows the lead of some colleges which provide extended time between semesters or report periods and encourage or require students to find jobs or do volunteer service. Focusing on all the community-based learning during a given week or month provides a welcome break in the academic schedule and frees the teachers to work on curriculum and evaluation. It also enables the school to continue the academic part of its program without interruption during the rest of the year. The drawback to such focused programs is that it is difficult to provide for and monitor the out-of-school learning of 150 students who are suddenly turned loose on a community. It also is difficult to find work and service opportunities for a short period of time for such a large number. And the very short period of a week or two, which some schools have experimented with, too often tempts students to use it as just another vacation.

A fourth approach is to restrict the community-based learning not to a single course but to some identifiable group. For example, many public schools are now stressing community-based learning for all seniors after college entrance decisions have been announced in April. Such programs are in response to the disease of "senioritis," the sharp drop in the motivation of seniors as they approach the end of their high school education.

Other schools screen and select students for community-based learning on the basis of a carefully developed proposal for study. In this approach the community-based learning is restricted to an elite group of students and consequently acquires significant prestige value. Such is the approach used in the Creative Studies Program in Abington (Pennsylvania) High School, where a limited number of highly motivated students are given time for community-based learning only after they have gone through careful screening procedures.

At the other extreme, many schools restrict community-based learning to the "troublemakers," using such programs as a way of getting students out of the school building into the community. Thus, a student with a long history of discipline trouble in school will be "encouraged" to leave school every day at noon to take a part-time job or perform volunteer service. While such attempts are often successful in helping the student tolerate an alien academic environment and in helping him or her learn significant skills, there are also some problems with such an approach. First, the program becomes stigmatized as a place for problem students. Second, the student who makes trouble for the school establishment often causes similar difficulties for his boss.

A final approach used by many schools is to permit each student to negotiate his own community-based learning on an individual basis. The school itself is not totally involved; no courses are specifically provided; and no special calendar breaks are set aside. Instead, students who are interested in community-based learning are given the encouragement and sanction to pursue it on their own. Such an approach is easiest for the school, since its only responsibility is for some minimal monitoring. Such an approach can also be said to replicate most closely the real-life experience of finding one's own job. One can thus argue that the approach will do the most to make the young person more independent.

However, its drawbacks are obvious. Most adolescents don't have the maturity to take such initiative. Their energies are expended for more immediate gratifications. And even those with the best of intentions find it difficult to locate and arrange for out-of-school learning. Also, such programs based solely on individual effort are difficult for school officials to monitor satisfactorily. Thus, to be successful, schools which wish to encourage individual students to begin community-based study should provide adult support and guidance, at least at the outset.

Through any of these approaches, alternative and conventional schools can begin to implement programs of community-based learning. If they do, what are the effects on the student? The evidence from the research is mixed. First, several studies indicate that there is no adverse effect on academic achievement, especially when the work is limited to not more than fifteen hours each week (Stromsdorfer, 1972). One survey of the research on affective growth reported that it "turned up little empirical evidence that action learning produces the affective growth in adolescents that theory predicts" (Graham, 1972, p. 77). There are, however, some clear effects on later employment. Students who have had extensive work experience during high school earn higher wages, report greater job satisfaction, and are less likely to be unemployed after high school graduation (Graham, 1972, p. 79).

Even though the research is somewhat inconclusive, the experience of alternative schools with community-based learning is positive enough that all secondary schools should implement some form of it. Such programs, it would seem, can best be implemented if steps similar to the following are taken.

1. The policy-making board of the school should establish basic policies concerning community-based learning: funding, staffing, crediting, evaluating, and so on.

2. The staff of the school, in consultation with interested students, should decide on the basic approach to be used, choosing from the approaches listed above or developing its own basic design.

3. Some type of advisory council should be formed, with strong representation from the business and labor communities. Parents, obviously, should also play an active part.

4. An extensive public relations campaign should be instituted so that the community is fully informed about the program and people who might be interested in cooperating are alerted.

5. A group of interested students, staff, and parents should make a complete canvass of the community, developing a card file of resources, listing people, places, and programs.

6. The program should then be introduced to the entire student body, preferably by a group of students who can encourage interested students to apply.

For every student engaged in community-based study, the school should require that a community-based learning contract be executed. While many students will consider this as unnecessary paperwork, it will do much to prevent later difficulties. The form should request such information as the following.

1. Student's name, address, telephone number, and
   school homeroom or counseling group.

2. Student's date of birth and Social Security number.
3. Brief description of the nature of the community-based learning.
4. Name and address of contact person in the community.
5. Number of hours each week student expects to spend on community-based learning.
6. Name of school staff member responsible for monitoring progress.
7. Brief description of how the student proposes that his or her community-based learning experience will be evaluated.
8. Any special costs or fees involved, with indication of who will pay such costs.
9. Type of school support which student will require for successful completion of community-based study (include people, materials, equipment and services).
10. Credits student hopes to earn, if any, through community-based study, with indication of number of credits and subject area to which they will be applied.
11. Amount and frequency of contact between school officials and student while student is involved in community-based study.
12. Anticipated learning outcomes to be derived from community-based study.
13. Parents' approval and signature.
14. Staff approval and signature.

In a sense this becomes a contract between the student and the school which clarifies in advance any areas of ambiguity and uncertainty. Such a contract can, of course, be modified so that it covers all types of community-based learning.

Ivan Illich (1970) and John Holt (1972) believe the community should be the center of learning. While the author is reluctant to embrace such a radical approach, he does feel that all students can be helped by some extensive use of the learning opportunities provided in any community.

References

Coleman, James S., et al. *Youth: Transition to Adulthood*. Chicago: University of Chicago Press, 1974.

Graham, Richard A. "Learning from Experience, a Preliminary Report," in *American Youth in the Mid-Seventies*. Washington, D.C.: National Association of Secondary School Principals, 1972, pp. 77, 79.

Havighurst, Robert J., Richard A. Graham, and Donald J. Eberly. "American Youth in the Mid-Seventies," in *American Youth in the Mid-Seventies*, Washington, D.C.: National Association of Secondary School Principals, 1972, p. 18.

Hebeisen, Ardyth. *Peer Program for Youth*. Minneapolis, Minnesota: Augsburg Publishing House, 1973.

Holt, John. *Freedom and Beyond*. New York: E. P. Dutton, 1972.

Illich, Ivan D. *Deschooling Society*. New York: Harper and Row, 1970.

"Resources for Youth," newsletter of the National Commission on the Resources of Youth, New York.

Stromsdorfer, E. "An Economic Analysis of the Work Experience and Career Exploration Program, 1970–1971," prepared for the U.S. Department of Labor, 1972.

Wurman, Richard S. (ed.). *Yellow Pages of Learning Resources*, Cambridge, Massachusetts: MIT Press, 1972.

CHAPTER SEVEN

Staffing, Teaching, Counseling: New Patterns

The old ideas about staffing a school, teaching a class, and counseling a student are being seriously challenged by the alternative schools movement. This chapter examines the reasons that such challenges have developed, surveys some prevailing patterns in alternative schools, and then recommends some options that alternative and conventional schools might consider.

A New Look at Staffing

Several reasons can be adduced for the development of new staffing patterns in alternative schools, and all are linked directly with the free school movement, which was the precursor of alternative schools.

The first was a distrust of bureaucracy and hierarchy, an expression of a democratic egalitarianism that rejected all authority except the authority of competence. There was among free school people a strong conviction, probably related to the anarchic sentiments of some of the free school gurus, that all hierarchy is evil. Here, for example, is H. Bennett, advising parents about starting a school:

> *Hierarchies and Other Dirty Words:* As soon as you move
> beyond the simplicity of the Minimal School, you face the problems

of developing workable systems for the necessary division of labor and responsibility. Along with the division of labor will come the creation of a hierarchy. Unless all this is approached in a direct manner, a "pecking order" takes over, with power struggles and injured egos building to create a major crisis. So approach this problem openly. Schedule regular meetings which include everyone that has anything to do with the day to day operation of the school [H. Bennett, 1972, pp. 82–83].

And the public school teachers who often started the public alternative were influenced not only by such free school rhetoric but also by their own bad experiences with hierarchical structures in the public school.

A second factor was a belief in the centrality of teaching. The free school movement saw learning in its purest form, stripping away from the learning encounter all the incrustations of coordinators, supervisors, and assistants developed by a self-perpetuating bureaucracy. All that was needed for learning to take place was a competent concerned person meeting with an interested learner; all the rest was superfluous. And leadership was seen only as a necessary evil. Here, for example, is the advice from *Rasberry Exercises*, one of the most influential "do-your-own-school" manuals:

> Someone granted power by the community [is needed], someone to make day-to-day decisions (within, of course, "policy" set down by the Board). Someone to free the teachers to float with the children *full time*. Isn't that what it's all about, learning, and loving? To be with someone you love *full time*, even when you know it's a short time? [All italics in original] [Rasberry and Greenway, 1970, pp. 15–17].

Among the public school alternative teachers, who often were the initiating force in alternative schools, this belief in the centrality of teaching might be seen as simply a projection of a naïve egocentrism, rather than a radically different view of learning and schooling. It was there, however, as a force to be reckoned with.

The final factor was the very mundane problem of lack of money. In the free school movement, "lack of money" meant the painful reality of having no money except that which was brought in by tuition. And the problems of raising even minimal funds just to pay the teachers a maintenance salary often divided free school people. Here, for example, is an excerpt from a free school "town meeting":

> JENNY: There are expenses, say several thousand dollars a year, to keep this school going. Is it fair if everybody can come and use the school equally, but only half the people are going to do the fund-raising and other work? You may say it's not free if we insist that everybody has to help keep the school alive, but if we don't insist on that, not everyone's going to help—and that sure as hell isn't fair.
>
> SANDRA: Everyone needs the money—the school needs it—but some people have not reached a level of consciousness where they are able to contribute something with an understanding of what the contribution means. That doesn't have to mean that because a person doesn't help in the Open House you're going to deny that person the right to come back to school next fall, does it? If indeed, by hook or by crook, you do manage to get the money to survive [Elizabeth Cleaners Street School, 1972, pp. 71, 73].

Money was needed simply to survive; there was never any question about spending it on counselors, coordinators, or anyone else except a teacher.

The public alternatives, of course, did not experience the same degree of penury. To public school teachers who began alternative schools, the message was typically received in this fashion: "Yes, you may begin an alternative school. But you can't spend more than we spend in the regular school." Since the most pressing concern from the teachers' point of view was to have small classes, the highest budget priority was for teaching staff and then teaching materials. All other paid personnel simply got crowded out.

So ideology, ego, and economics have forced us to take a fresh look at how we staff schools. And public alternatives have come up with some interesting patterns. The answers found by public alternative schools will be examined here through the classifications of leadership, instruction, and counseling.

Administrative Structures

Alternative schools have experimented with a variety of administrative and leadership structures. The particular leadership structure used seems to be most affected by the size of the unit, the relationship with the other schools, and local district practices.

Perhaps the most common pattern, at least among the larger autonomous alternative schools, is to have a full-time director or coordinator. This person comes to the job from a variety of routes. Many are chosen from the ranks of teachers interested in the school; some are selected from a nationwide search; a few come from the ranks of district administrators. Although some, like Wayne Jennings of the St. Paul Open School, use the title of "principal," the most common title among the full-time people is "director." Most of the directors who have talked about their role see it as a full-time position, even in small schools, for the alternative school director typically suffers from what the sociologists call role overload. It is not unusual for the director to teach, counsel, provide instructional leadership, develop curriculum, work with colleges, handle public relations, arrange bus schedules, take care of visitors, and handle correspondence. And the author personally recalls that his first task every morning upon arriving at Alternative East was to sweep out the office and make the coffee.

In the smaller schools and in the alternative programs, the most common title is "head teacher." There are, of course, some titular variations: the Mini-School of Julia Richman High School in New York City has a "teacher-in-charge"; the John Bowne Prep School, also in New York City, has a "teacher–coordinator." Regardless of the title, the implication is clear: the person is a member of the teaching staff who has been given special coordinating responsibilities. Usually, this individual continues to teach a few classes and provides a less directive leadership; the title "coordinator" or "head teacher" usually connotes a role with less authority than a principal or director. The head teacher position also seems to involve a shorter tenure than does the position of director.

Occasionally, in alternative schools there is a dual leadership structure. In the early years of the West Philadelphia Free School, for example, there was an "inside man" and an "outside man." The inside man was responsible for internal affairs of materials, curriculum, instruction, discipline. The outside man handled external affairs—community relationships, university contacts, parent problems, visitors, police, and the like. Such a dual leadership structure does not usually persist; invariably, one or the other assumes more control, and the counterpart plays assistant.

A relatively small number of alternatives operate with some type of committee leadership. The Village School in Great Neck, New York, describes its leadership pattern in this way:

Students and teachers share equal responsibility for fashioning the policies and organization of the school. An executive committee composed of the faculty and an equal number of selected students is charged with running the school, but larger policy decisions are still determined at general meetings where all participants may attend and vote [From a program description supplied by the school, no date or authorship specified].

The Cambridge Pilot School in Massachusetts has actively experimented with different types of leadership. The program began with dual coordinators. For the third year the school hired a full-time director and assistant director; during the fourth year there was a full-time director assisted by a Harvard Graduate School of Education fellow. Both individuals were affiliated with and supported by Harvard. At this writing there is one administrator, called an acting dean, who is on the payroll of the Cambridge school district.

The reporting relationships get complicated. The typical pattern in alternative programs is for the head teacher to be responsible to the principal of the main school. Even in a city like Philadelphia, where there is a district office for alternative programs, the local alternative head reports to the principal, not to the district office. Leonard Finkelstein, director of the

Philadelphia alternative programs, indicated that one of the factors in the success of Philadelphia's program was this clear and direct relationship; the building principal feels a close and supportive relationship with "his" alternative. Philadelphia now has close to one hundred alternative programs, and Finkelstein feels that this organizational structure has facilitated a rapid and healthy growth (Conversation with author).

In the autonomous alternative school, the director has more independence and usually reports directly to a district superintendent. This relationship is found, for example, in the School Without Walls of Washington, D.C., where a principal heads a staff of five teachers and eleven off-campus instructors. In alternative schools that serve several school districts, like the Alternative Schools Project of suburban Philadelphia, the director usually reports to a policy-making board composed of representatives from the several districts. In the case of this particular alternative program, the policy board includes an interesting cross section: one superintendent, one school board member, one teacher, one parent, and one student from each of the six districts.

Regardless of the type of administrative structure, most alternative school people seem to agree that some type of full-time on-site autonomous leadership is essential. And all of these factors seem important: full-time because the job is a complicated and demanding one, on-site because the remote leader loses influence and gets out-of-touch, and autonomous because accountability is possible only if authority is clear and unambiguous.

New Approaches to Counseling

In examining the need for alternative path counseling for dropouts, the Syracuse Policy Institute concluded:

> Without denigrating the work of the present school counselors, who are usually overburdened with a wide variety of counseling and administrative tasks, one is forced to conclude that most potential drop-outs cannot enjoy trusting and intensive counseling services in existing school systems. Many students in trouble avoid their counselors. They cannot be sure their discussions with coun-

selors will not be reported to school and community authorities for disciplinary purposes [Bailey, Macy, and Vickers, 1973, p. 48].

The same study reports that the average counselor–student ratio, nationally, is 1 to 450, an impossible burden for any counselor.

In an attempt to deal with the problem of overworked and out-of-touch counselors, alternative schools have tried three different patterns.

When the alternative program is housed in the regular school, the counselor often becomes an advocate and defender. Earl E. Avery, counselor assisting at Small House in Ann Arbor, Michigan, sees these tasks becoming central for the alternative school counselor:

> The implication is clear. The counselor becomes the advocate for the student and, eventually, a defender of the program. The role of the guidance counselor in the genesis of Small House involved advocating and now involves defending to those who question it. As the program progresses, the role of the counselor extends in many directions [Avery, 1973, pp. 55–56].

Other role redefinition occurs when the alternative school adds a counselor to the staff and makes him or her an integral part of the instructional team. The smallness of the alternative school means that even a counselor who chooses to function in a traditional one-to-one fashion is able to keep in close touch with almost the entire student population. And in such a situation, the counselor perforce is thrust into different roles —teaching classes, working with small groups, maintaining contact with parents. The Berkeley (California) Model School A uses a full-time counselor in such a fashion.

In those alternative schools dealing with special student populations, the counselor assumes a central role, becoming a nucleus around which the rest of the staff is built. At The Cottage in Seattle, Washington, which developed as an alternative within the Rainiér Beach High School, a counseling component was built into the program as a major thrust. And in the Urban Career Education Center in Philadelphia, where the school's concern is for career education in an alternative setting, the counseling staff plays a central role, with an active group of counselors serving the needs of 150 teen-agers.

At the other extreme, most alternative schools have developed a new role of teacher–counselor. The approach used at the Alternative Schools Project seems representative of alternative school practice: each student selects a "support teacher" from among the staff; the support teacher works with the students individually and in small groups to help with course selection, assist in the college admissions game, work out problems within the school, and lend a sympathetic ear to students with problems. The system seems to work, according to an interim evaluation of the support-teacher concept at the Alternative Schools Project: "The conclusions warranted by these data are obvious: a large majority of all students, regardless of sub-group or need set, are deriving satisfaction from their support relationships. The data clearly indicate that student needs, as diverse as they may be, are being met through the support relationships" (Gibboney and Langsdorf, 1973, pp. 24–25).

The Worcester Alternative School in Massachusetts is very explicit about the role of the teacher–adviser:

Each student in the Worcester Alternative School has an adviser from the regular staff of the school. The relationship will be one of mutual respect and negotiation. Advisers will be assigned at the beginning of the year and while little need to do so is foreseen, changes in advisers can be made during the year in special cases with the consent of all persons involved. The functions of the adviser system will be as follows:

1. To be the primary basis for evaluation of the student's overall program of learning experiences.

2. To provide for a close relationship with at least one staff member within the organizational framework of the school.

3. To help the student in choosing learning experiences and for setting up part or the whole of his or her program.

4. To provide a link between the student, the learning experience, and the school system as a whole.

5. To place responsibility between staff and student in a personal and helping relationship rather than a structural or organizational one.

6. To provide a personal basis for the questions of promotion, graduation, and/or status in the school.

7. To provide a link between parents, the school, and the student's work.

8. To provide a link between the student, a community learning experience, and the school ["Year Two Catalog," 1973, p. 8].

Cambridge Pilot School has experimented with a team-advising system. One teacher, one parent or community volunteer, one teacher intern, and one student member work with advising groups of twenty-two on a continuing basis. Such a diversified team would seem to provide maximum support for the students, and Patrick Pietrovito's observations of the counseling and advising system in action at Pilot indicate that there were evident signs of success (Pietrovito, "Cambridge Pilot School," unpublished observation report, 1973).

However, there have been problems with the teacher–adviser system; at the Alternative Schools Project the parents ranked counseling as the fourth most critical problem (Gibboney and Langsdorf, 1973, p. 153). Students and parents at other alternative schools have expressed similar concerns, citing lack of consistent contact, confusing advice, and the unavailability of the teacher–adviser or counselor.

The author's own observations and discussions with alternative school people lead him to believe that the teacher–counselor program can work effectively if the alternative school or program follows certain important steps:

1. Provide the staff with systematic in-service work on the new role and the competencies required, with special attention being paid to group process skills.

2. Permit the students to choose their own teacher–counselor and to change their counselor any time at all.

3. Provide the staff and students with a good supply of materials designed to facilitate self-directed guidance. Excellent materials for college selection, career choice, and personal

adjustment are available (see, for example, *The Self-Directed Search*, by John Holland, 1971, which enables the student to do his or her own career counseling).

4. Schedule the students to meet with the counselor–teacher once or twice a week on a regular basis, with academic credit for the sessions, and with whatever attendance controls the school sees fit to impose.

5. With the staff develop an explicit statement of the teacher–counselor role, making clear the role expectations.

The author believes that such steps will ensure a counseling program that will have a much higher degree of effectiveness than any conventional guidance program.

Teaching

Alternative schools have experimented with new approaches to instructional staffing by finding new relationships, new concepts, new people, and new roles.

The new relationships have grown out of the teachers' need to work together both to provide new resources for the student and to mitigate the isolation that the teacher often feels. The team-teaching approaches advocated long ago by such innovators as J. Lloyd Trump (see, for example, his pioneering work *Images of the Future*, 1959) have been expanded by many alternative schools; instead of simply being ways to realign the staff, these team-teaching approaches have also facilitated new approaches to the curriculum. At the Wilson Campus School at Mankato State College in Minnesota, staff members are organized into several thematic teams. One team, for example, is the "critical issues" team, which organizes two phases of learning. The first is composed of mini-courses and independent studies. The second is the "crucial issues experience" held off campus. As described by the school, "Goals of value clarification, social consciousness will be accomplished through student participation in human relations strategies, in simulations, and in community action projects" (Walker, 1973, p. 12).

The critical issues are determined by the students and in the past have included political elections, drugs, the draft, population, racism, and sexism.

As noted in Chapter 5, such realignments of teaching staffs often come about from the frustration of offering unrelated mini-courses. Whereas the standard team-teaching plan in the sixties was usually the result of an administrative mandate for some structural innovation, the team efforts in alternative schools more often than not are a grass-roots phenomenon. Three or four teachers get together and say, "Instead of offering mini-courses, let's work together around some common theme or idea. What do you think we could teach together?" They are individuals in search of a group, then a group in search of a goal.

Alternative schools have also expanded the notions of what a teacher is and does. There is, of course, the expected rhetoric that talks about the teacher as facilitator and supportive resource. But most alternative teachers have gone beyond that rhetoric in two ways. First, in addition to teaching classes, alternative school teachers have taken on many noninstructional jobs: finding community resources, developing curricula, participating in decision making, counseling students, arranging and supervising survival expeditions, recruiting students, meeting with hostile civic groups, and politicking for funds. They take on so many extra tasks, in fact, that they overextend themselves. Robert Riordan wisely advances this cautionary note:

> Staff members expend enormous amounts of energy on a variety of tasks, ranging from service on a curriculum committee to course planning to evaluation to individual tutoring and counseling; the "hang-loose" principle often leads to role confusion and inconsistency in personal interactions. The diffusion of energy on a variety of unrelated tasks leads to the phenomenon of "burning out," as teachers and students retreat into more constricted roles [Riordan, 1972, p. 40].

This same concern was expressed more poignantly to the author by a teacher in the Alternative Schools Project who mused,

"Why do I work my ass off so some sixteen-year-old kid can have a groovy time?"

Second, in their instructional role many alternative teachers find themselves working differently. There is no standard "alternative style," and alternative teachers do not have a monopoly on instructional innovation. However, observations indicate that alternative teachers spend more time than teachers in conventional schools helping students clarify goals, working collaboratively with students in identifying resources, involving students in shaping the curriculum, assisting students in developing group structures, providing resources for students to work independently. Conversely, alternative teachers seem to spend less time lecturing, testing, checking roll, scolding, and conducting a recitation.

This does not suggest that alternative teachers see themselves only as "facilitators" and "resources." The most successful teachers in alternative schools are basically like the most successful teachers in conventional schools: they are competent adults who care about young people, are enthusiastic about what they know, and are able to transmit both competency and enthusiasm to those they teach. Many alternative school teachers report that they had to learn that lesson the hard way. They entered the alternative school feeling that the setting required them to deny their hard-won skills in order to play the role of "friendly facilitator," only to be rejected by students who were demanding authentic competency. One student at the Alternative School remarked impatiently to the author about one of his teachers: "For two weeks now I've been sitting in class, and all that guy does is ask what we think. I'd like to know for a change what the hell he thinks."

New people have been brought into the alternative schools as a way of increasing instructional resources, reducing costs, and providing adult diversity. The staff at Marshall-University (Minneapolis) High School is typical; it includes principal, teachers, counselor, community volunteers, student teachers, university interns, and paraprofessionals. Perhaps the most important contribution made by alternative schools comes about from this willingness to experiment boldly with the concept "teacher." It is not unusual for the entire staff to be pressed into service: the director's secretary teaches typing, the custodian instructs in home repair, the director teaches a course in "Plato" and "Clipper Ships," as John Bremer did when he was director of Parkway. Any competent person in the community may be enlisted. Artists, plumbers, doctors, veterinarians, automobile mechanics either come to the school to do their thing or have the students come to them. Finally, students themselves either teach regular courses or participate in skill exchanges, informal arrangements whereby student teaches student.

Another approach to diversifying the instructional staff is the use of part-time, noncertificated people. The author found during his tenure at the Alternative Schools Project that he could recruit an outstanding group of people who were willing to teach for eight dollars an hour. And he used a marketplace decision-making process as a way of selecting staff. Anyone who wanted to teach on a part-time basis would appear at a stated time in the assembly area, set up a small table, pass out a dittoed sheet describing himself or herself and the course, and try to sell the course. Any course that drew more than ten enrollees had a good chance of being supported by the student–faculty curriculum committee.

Such arrangements have not always met with support from teachers' associations and teachers' unions. The attitude of Albert Shanker and the United Federation of Teachers (UFT) has been somewhat ambivalent. Shanker is clearly on record as supporting options within the system (*New York Times*, December 21, 1970), but the UFT has strongly opposed the use of noncertificated teachers in Harlem Prep. Harlem Prep, which was one of the most successful "freedom schools" of the late sixties, became part of the New York City public school system in 1974. Although Harlem Prep officials reported that they anticipated no changes in the school program or staffing, UFT representatives informed a *Christian Science Monitor* reporter that the federation opposed the use of noncertificated people

(*Christian Science Monitor*, March 11, 1974).

In a time of a teacher surplus, such an attitude on the part of professional associations is quite reasonable and understandable; teachers' associations are justifiably concerned that new approaches to staffing could result in a net decrease in employment opportunities for teachers. There is, however, a solution which many alternative schools have found workable: at the outset enlist the support of the teachers' group and build in guarantees that nonconventional staffing patterns will not reduce the number of positions available for certificated people. As pointed out earlier, Philadelphia has been able to open close to one hundred alternative programs, all staffed by full-fledged members of the teachers' union. Finkelstein encourages his staff to work with union representatives, not to see them as adversaries (Conversation with author).

Finally, the instructional staffs of alternative schools have been supplemented with new staff roles. In many alternative schools the people doing the staffing have put aside conventional notions about who is needed to staff a school and have focused instead on the needs of the youth—and have found some new ways of responding to those needs with some different kinds of people.

One new role found most often in alternative schools is a person who coordinates community placements. As greater emphasis was placed on community involvement, the staffing personnel found that they needed someone to locate community resources, to explain the program's objectives to community people, to inform students of community opportunities, to arrange for community placement, and to follow up so that problems could be anticipated or solved when they developed. Patrick Pietrovito, who observed the community coordinator in New Haven's (Connecticut) High School at work in the community, stressed the importance of the coordinator's follow-up work:

> The coordinator tries to maintain phone contact with the resource person every two weeks. He tries to see students more frequently to check on their progress and their feelings toward the

placement. At the end of the placement, the community resource person is asked to meet with the student and develop an evaluation of the student's progress based on his pre-established goals. . . . The coordinator tries to develop a pattern or history of student and resource person response [Patrick Pietrovito, "Community Orientation Program of the High School in the Community," unpublished report, 1973].

Schools that recruit dropouts are using street-wise young adults to make initial contacts, to help adolescents find their way in the urban jungle, to snoop out and prevent destructive conflict, and to serve as a liaison between teachers and parents. Two schools that have supplemented the instructional staff with such street workers are Haaren High School's mini-schools and the John Bowne Prep School (both in New York City). Under a grant from the Ford Foundation, these schools have found the street worker an important part of the school's community program.

Alternative schools have found that other special needs also require special staff. The Off-Campus School in Bellevue, Washington, uses a learning disabilities teacher on a half-time basis. And the Alternative Schools Project in suburban Philadelphia employed two full-time specialists in disabilities when that school included handicapped students in its program. Both specialists, by all staff reports, performed a very vital function and were able to help the staff work more effectively with a variety of students.

One important difference in the alternative's use of such specialists is that they are most often a fully integrated part of the teaching staff, without special authority or status, and often spend as much time as the rest of the teaching staff in teaching, counseling, sweeping up, making coffee, and doing the dishes.

Matching Teacher and Student

Besides trying to find new ways of organizing and staffing, alternative schools have also explored some methods for matching students with teachers. The concern for matching student with teacher stems from a threefold commitment: the belief that students should have a choice of teachers, the conviction that there is no single best kind of teaching, and the hope that there may be some optimal fit between student and teacher.

Such beliefs are, of course not original with alternative schools. Herbert Thelen as early as 1957 was exploring ways of grouping students for "teachability," matching students and teachers who preferred each other. His study, concluded in 1960 but not published until 1967, produced these findings:

> Given classes composed of more "teachable" students, the teachers on the average had more orderly and manageable classes; they tended to like the students better; they gave them better grades. The "teachable" students tended to like the teacher only slightly more than did the control students, they gained no more on achievement tests, and they tended to express a higher level of satisfaction with the activities and with the course as a whole. They also tended to like each other better and by and large the teachable classes had greater solidarity than did the control classes [Thelen, 1967, p. 185].

David E. Hunt of the Ontario Institute for Studies in Education is testing another model based upon the student's conceptual complexity or interpersonal maturity. Hunt has identified three stages through which the child passes: Stage A, immature, unsocialized; Stage B, dependent and conforming; Stage C, self-reliant. He has identified the learner characteristics for each level and posited the most facilitative teaching methods and procedures for each respective level. At the time of writing, his model was being tested in one elementary and one junior high school. (For a description of his approach, see the paper by Hunt, Greenwood, and Brill, 1972.)

Mario D. Fantini suggests three basic teaching styles —structured, modified, and informal—which would fit three kinds of environments. Fantini describes them in this fashion:

> 1. This option [structured] could provide a learning environment which is primarily teacher-controlled. A school incorporating some of the ideas of the Classic School or the Structured School with Student Input could create this environment. 2. This option

[modified] could provide a learning environment which would receive direction from both teacher and student, but for the most part would be teacher-controlled. A school incorporating some ideas of the Modular School or the Individualized Instruction School might create this environment. 3. This option [informal] could provide a learning environment where teachers and students together would plan the learning experience. A school incorporating these ideas of Project to Individualize Education or the Open School could create this environment [Fantini, 1973, p. 73].

Most alternative schools do not get involved with the complex schemes proposed by these researchers. Typically, the alternative school lists a course with a teacher's name and lets the student choose the teacher, depending on the student grapevine to spread the word about "good" and "poor," "hard" and "easy" teachers. Worcester Alternative School goes beyond this; each teacher lists the subjects he teaches and his interests in the course booklet. Here, for example, is one typical listing:

> Frank ——— . Art-Communication Team.
> Subjects teaching: Elementary and Advanced Spanish
> Health and Nutrition
> U. S. History
> Interests: Physical education, body awareness, exercises, music listening, yoga and concentration, meditation, agriculture, (organic) religion (particularly Far Eastern), chess, education, and relaxation ["Year Two Catalog," 1973, p. 6].

The author thinks the matter of matching is important, but he believes there are solutions available that are less complex than the Hunt approach and perhaps more effective than Worcester's. His proposal is, first of all, based upon a simple continuum of teacher characteristics. He has selected characteristics that seem most important to students, based upon discussion with students, observations, and reading of the literarure. As Table 7 indicates, he has identified ten such characteristics and labeled them in terms that students can understand. Four of these—organization, discipline, distance, and mood—relate directly to the matter of classroom climate, an important element in the students' attitudes. The other six

—tests, pace, homework, grading, facts, and concern—have to do with instructional practices and speak of "teaching style" in terms that a student can understand. While the instrument has not yet been validated in any systematic studies, the author believes that it will be useful in facilitating student–teacher matching.

Each of these characteristics is represented by a continuum, with the extremes identified by contrasting words. Insofar as possible prejudicial value loadings have been avoided; if the words on the left seem somehow more positive in their loading, that reflects only the bias of the current rhetoric, not any reality about the effective teacher. Between these two extreme terms are six points on a scale, representing shadings along that continuum.

Perhaps a few of the terms need clarification. "Organization" refers to the teacher's lesson planning and curricular structure: the "loose" teacher is more concerned with spontaneity and impromptu use of the moment; the "organized" teacher is concerned with sequential planning, articulation, careful linking of lessons. "Distance" refers to the psychic distance between teacher and student preferred by the teacher. "Mood" refers to the teacher's characteristic affect. "Facts" re-

Table 7 The "Here I Am" Teacher Continuum

Element	Limit						Limit
Organization	Loose	o	o	o	o	o	o	Organized
Discipline	Easy	o	o	o	o	o	o	Strict
Distance	Close	o	o	o	o	o	o	Apart
Mood	Funny	o	o	o	o	o	o	Serious
Tests	Unimportant	o	o	o	o	o	o	Important
Pace	Slow	o	o	o	o	o	o	Fast
Homework	Little	o	o	o	o	o	o	Much
Grading	Easy	o	o	o	o	o	o	Hard
Facts	Unimportant	o	o	o	o	o	o	Important
Concern	Student	o	o	o	o	o	o	Subject

fers to the teacher's concern with cognitive memory and recall of factual information. "Concern" is a broad term referring to whether the teacher sees himself or herself as concerned primarily with student or with subject.

The plan proposed is a simple one. At the start of the year, the director discusses the scale with the teachers and students, stressing that there is no value loading and emphasizing the need for insight and self-awareness. The director fills out a form for himself or herself, modeling the behavior he or she desires. The staff and students discuss the characteristics in small groups, talking informally about the kinds of teachers preferred. Each staff member then puts an X on the continuum to represent his or her self-perception. The teacher then posts this scale on the classroom door or on some central bulletin board. Students who have worked with the teacher are encouraged to use a check mark to show how they perceive the teacher, thus giving the teacher some useful feedback. Then during the registration process, copies of each teacher's scale are included in the course booklet, and students are able to select the kind of teacher they prefer for each subject.

The scale has several advantages. First, it focuses on teacher characteristics important to students. Second, it is phrased in a way that communicates simply to students and teachers. Third, it attempts to be nonjudgmental. Fourth, it is dynamic; the teacher is encouraged to make out a new chart any time he or she feels there has been a change. Finally, it provides some useful feedback to the teacher from the students.

Through some such process as this schools can very simply establish more teachable climates.

Putting It All Together

How can an alternative school use all these ideas in a comprehensive plan for staffing? Although the author prefers a situation where each school develops several alternative staffing patterns of its own, he would like to advance a model for consideration.

First, the planning group begins with some general idea of the target population—the students for whom the school will be designed. Which students will the alternative try to serve? What are their general characteristics? What are their priority needs? What type of school can best serve those needs? Out of this kind of needs assessment, the planning group makes some tentative decisions about program emphases. Later on, when the staff is selected, it will shape the actual program itself; these discussions are only preliminary. On the basis of these preliminary decisions about program, the planning group is ready to select the staff.

The rationale for such a process should be stressed. One does not begin with some bias about what kinds of people are needed; one begins instead with some idea of the population to be served, the program to be developed—and then makes some kind of determination about the staff needs. If, for example, the planning group decides it needs a school for dropouts, the group develops some tentative program ideas—affective education, career studies, work–study plan, basic skills component, perhaps. The group then decides on the kind of staff required, within the constraints of the budget.

The group then works up a staffing table for the school, based upon a tentative identification of students and a preliminary decision about the program. The planning group decides on the priority staff needs and then decides how that staff can be supplemented with specialists and ancillary personnel. Let's take an example and see how an alternative school can use resources more effectively.

Let's posit a conventional high school with a student population of 1,000, with the following staffing budget. (Note: administrative salaries and salaries for nurses, librarians, cafeteria workers, custodians, and so on are excluded.)

3 guidance counselors (1 counselor for 330 students)	$ 36,000	($12,000 each)
6 department chairmen (teach half-time)	78,000	(13,000 each)

47	teachers (with chair- men, they make an effective staff of 50)	470,000	(10,000 each)
	Total	$584,000	

With these fifty teachers the average class size is twenty; the counselor–student ratio, as noted above, is 1–330.

Now the principal tells an alternative planning group something like this: "Plan an alternative school for a turned-off blue-collar working-class group. You will get about 166 students and can have one-sixth of the instructional budget, or about $97,000." The planning group decides it wants a program stressing basic skills and community involvement, with a heavy component of physical education. So the group develops a staffing model that looks like this:

1	head teacher, teaching half-time, preferably industrial arts background	$13,000	
5	teachers—1 English, 1 math, 1 social studies, 1 science, 1 physical education	50,000	
900	hours of part-time instruction, enough for 3 hours a week, 30 weeks, 10 courses throughout the year—equivalent of 2 teachers	7,200	($8 hourly)
1	community coordinator, half-time	6,000	
10	half-time teaching interns	0	
10	half-time volunteers	0	
1	reading specialist, full-time	12,000	
1	math specialist, half-time	6,000	
	Total	$94,200	

Total instructional staff equivalents: 20

So the alternative school, with a comparable budget, has a more powerful staff and is able to reduce class size by one-half. The school sets up eight advising teams, reducing counseling ratios to 1 to 21.

With some general staffing patterns like this in mind, the planners select the students and then begin to recruit staff. Here the recommendation is that the planners make a clear statement of the school's mission and invite anyone to apply who wants to support that mission. The proposed school for dropouts might advertise like this:

> We are planning a no-nonsense alternative school for blue-collar dropouts. We want teachers who understand the life-style of poor kids, black and white. We want to run a program that is flexible, has a strong affective component, and helps kids find jobs. But we will not be a free school. Our goal is to be tough and tender—to work with the kids in setting reasonable limits and to enforce those limits rather closely. We need one take-charge head teacher who doesn't object to structure and five teachers who know the usual school stuff but who also have other competencies. If you think you'd like to work with us, give us a call.

Such a clear statement about goals would avoid dysfunctional goal conflicts. Yet it also gives teachers freedom of choice without categorizing them; it should also result in a rather significant measure of staff diversity. Once the teachers are hired, they can then identify themselves according to the rubric suggested above and let the students select their teachers wherever a choice is feasible.

A plan of this sort provides the maximum amount of flexibility, the greatest number of staff resources, and the largest measure of option and freedom for students and teachers.

References

Avery, Earl E. "The Small House Concept: The Role of the Guidance Counselor," in *Alternative Education in a Pluralistic Society*, edited by Charles D. Moody, Charles B. Vergon, and Jean Leonard. Ann Arbor: University of Michigan Press, 1973.

Bailey, Stephen K., Francis V. Macy, and Donn F. Vickers. *Alternative Paths to the High School Diploma*. Syracuse, New York: Syracuse University Research Corporation, 1973

Bennett, H. *No More Public School*. New York: Random House, 1972.

Elizabeth Cleaners Street School. *Starting Your Own School*. New York: Random House, 1972.

Fantini, Mario D. *Public Schools of Choice*. New York: Simon and Schuster, 1973.

Gibboney, Richard A., and Michael G. Langsdorf. "Interim Evaluation Report for the Alternative School Project, 1972–73." Philadelphia: Educational Development Center, University of Pennsylvania, 1973.

Holland, John L. *The Self-Directed Search*. Palo Alto, California: Consulting Psychologists Press, 1971.

Hunt, David E., Jo Ann Greenwood, and Ronald Brill. "From Psychological Theory to Educational Practice: Implementation of a Matching Model," Paper presented at American Educational Research Association Symposium, "Models of Teaching and Learning," April 7, 1972.

Rasberry, Salli, and Robert Greenway. *Rasberry Exercises: How to Start Your Own School and Make a Book*. Freestone, California: Freestone Publishing, 1970.

Riordan, Robert C. *Alternative Schools in Action*. Bloomington, Indiana: Phi Delta Kappa Educational Foundation, 1972.

Thelen, Herbert. *Classroom Grouping for Teachability*. New York: John Wiley, 1967.

Trump, J. Lloyd. *Images of the Future*. Washington: National Education Association, 1959.

Walker, Penelope. *Public Alternative Schools*. Amherst, Massachusetts: University of Massachusetts, 1973.

"Year Two Catalog of Possibilities, 1973–74," Worcester, Massachusetts: Worcester Alternative High School, 1973.

CHAPTER EIGHT

Evaluating
Student Learning During the past ten years
there has been a marked increase in educators' finding new
ways to evaluate student learning and to report student progress. As perhaps could have been expected, the alternative
schools have been in the forefront of this movement. If it made
sense to change the school organization and the school curriculum, it obviously made sense to develop new forms of
marking and grading. This chapter examines the reasons those
changes developed, reviews some new grading methods used
in the schools, and proposes an alternative system for consideration.

Reasons for the Interest in New Grading Systems

The need to develop better grading systems has long been
obvious to researchers, but not to practitioners. As early as
1911 Johnson demonstrated the diversity of standards within
departments of a high school and challenged the assumptions
behind the percentage grading systems so widely used. His
studies, as well as those by Rugg (1918) and others, encouraged
educators to move toward a system in which symbols represented and replaced percentage equivalents. By the end of the
twenties, 80 percent of the schools in Billett's study (1933)
reported the use of a letter grading system to record student
achievement. Despite continued research on the inadequacy of

letter grades, however, most schools have retained some form of letter grades to represent the complex matter of student learning and growth. For fifty years, then, the grading system has remained relatively unchanged, except for isolated and sporadic attempts to improve it.

Why, then, has there been more experimentation in the past ten years, with several serious attempts to find new approaches? There probably are three reasons that can be adduced.

The first is a marked change in attitudes among the young. Part of the rhetoric of the counter-culture was a rejection of competition and the reward–punishment system based upon competition. There was instead a concomitant valuing of cooperation, of not making a peer look bad by "getting ahead" of him or her. Typical of many such protests about the grading system was this statement of a "blueprint of high school reform" by two students from Elgin (Illinois) High School:

> Grading and Testing: Goal—to remove the pressure of grade-level ranking which can cause cheating, shattered nerves, and hypertension.
> A. Pass-fail system of grading, the only pressure of which would be to obtain the knowledge to pass, thereby relieving the pressure on students to perform well in required courses which the student often deems irrelevant.
> B. Elimination of all testing on the national and state level: no IQ's, standardized tests, achievement tests; gear testing to local educational level [Divoky, 1969, p. 103].

A graduate student saw it this way:

> If grades do motivate, then they reinforce a value scheme that equates acceptability of self with performing better than others, that posits the belief that private rewards must and should come at the expense of others. The logical outcome of such a value system is precisely the war mentality of the "big, competitive world" [Martinez, 1968, p. 5].

A second factor in the interest in new approaches has been mounting evidence that the present system is not very effective. Hoyt's study of the relationship between grades in school and adult achievement concluded in this fashion: "Present evidence strongly suggests that college grades bear little or no relationship to any measures of adult accomplishment" (Hoyt, 1965, p. 45). Pallett (1965) found no relationship between college grades and ratings on any of the eight dimensions that characterized success in business. Barr's study (1961) showed that there was no relationship between grade point average as a predictor of success in teaching. Singer (1964) discovered a significant correlation between the grades men got and their manipulativeness, between the grades women got and their attractiveness. Numerous other studies indicated lack of consistency between how teachers graded the same set of essay papers, low correlations of creativity and high grade-point average, and the difficulty of interpreting reliably what a given grade represented from school to school. (For an excellent summary of the research on grading, see Kirschenbaum, Simon, and Napier, 1971.)

A final factor in this renewed interest in changing the grading system has been the attacks of educational critics who saw the weaknesses of the grading system and encouraged teachers and students to change it. Typical is this advice by Postman and Weingartner:

> Probably the most formidable obstacle to change in the schools is the grading system. Just about everyone who is part of a school knows this, including teachers. And yet no one seems to be able to get very far in disposing of grades. . . . If you can persuade your parents that the grading system is harmful, that it is actually depriving you of an authentic education, then you may also be able to persuade them to initiate a lawsuit against the school system, in which they contend that (1) a grade is a public document . . . (2) it is not the function of a school to make public evaluations of a student's behavior . . . (3) a bad grade constitutes a libelous statement . . . (4) a permanent injunction should be issued against the school to prevent it from making known, in any form, the results of student performance to anyone except the students and his parents [Postman and Weingartner, 1971, p. 113].

By the end of the sixties, then, there was a readiness to explore significantly new ways of grading and reporting. And the publication of the book *Wad-ja-get?* by Kirschenbaum, Simon, and Napier (1971), a fictionalized account of how a school changed its grading system, probably served as a catalyst in helping many schools actually make a change. As of this writing, the book has sold more than 50,000 copies, has given rise to the Center for Grading Alternatives (Upper Jay, New York), and has led to several national conferences on grading alternatives, attended by more than 2,000 school people. (Data above are based on telephone conversation with Howard Kirschenbaum, director of the Center for Grading Alternatives.) At the present time practically every alternative school is using some alternative form of grading, and according to some authoritative estimates, about one-third of conventional high schools are similarly experimenting.

New Grading Systems

What new systems have alternative schools developed? This section will examine in some depth the evaluation systems used by several representative alternative schools and then make some general observations concerning such systems.

The Parma City Schools (Cleveland) Education Through Inquiry program (ETI) combines a pass-fail marking system with a periodic progress report. The progress report is given to the student and the parents four or five weeks into the program, and the pass-fail report at the end of nine weeks. The progress report includes a "progress grade," a report on the number of absences, a teacher's comment about progress, and the teacher's specific suggestions as to how improvement can be effected. The progress report is prepared in triplicate, with one copy going to the student and parent, one for the teacher, and one for the counselor. The student may take the pass-fail option for only one credit each year; the student must choose the option and the course by the sixth week of school, must get parental approval, and must meet all requirements of the course to get the passing grade. Pass-fail marks are not averaged for grade-point average or class rank.

In the Shaker Heights (Ohio) Catalyst program, the student begins by developing a "contractual agreement." The contractual agreement requires the student to supply the following information: title of project, general area of studies, amount of credit desired, clock hour credit expectations, general scope of the project, preferred method of evaluation (pass-fail or letter grade), how project will be evaluated, what the student expects to learn, and arrangements for seminar group. The contract is signed by the adult who has agreed to sponsor the project. Each month of the project, the project sponsor completes an "initial student evaluation," in which the following questions are asked:

Does the student seem really to want to grow in the area of his project?

Is your relationship with the student smooth, or are there obvious tensions?

Does the student have specific habits which please or bother you? If so, please list them.

Are there any emotional conditions which either help or hinder the student? Please elaborate.

Describe the work done and gains made by the student during the past month.

The sponsor also completes a final evaluation of the student's project.

The New School of Cleveland Heights–University Heights (Ohio) grants a student credit for a course on the basis of a student journal, a course sheet, and a student evaluation form. In the journal the student records the learning experience for that week, the time spent, and the proportional number of credit hours requested for the work performed. The student and his or her home-group adviser periodically assign a letter grade for each full unit of credit earned; letter grades are given unless the student opts for "pass-fail" or "satisfactory-unsatisfactory" instead.

The Pilot School in Cambridge, Massachusetts, has explored several different grading systems, finally choosing a letter grade with a written comment. Director Ray F. Shurtleff explained the staff's decision in this way:

> The position of a combination of letter grades and written comments has always won out, because of very real institutional constraints: if a student transferred back to one of the regular high schools, there had to be a numerical grade attached to pass-fail courses; college admissions officers preferred a majority of letter or numerical grades on a transcript and a desire on the part of many students and parents to receive "grades" in addition to written evaluations [Shurtleff, 1973, p. 80].

In each class the staff and students together determine the procedures for evaluation, so that the threat of a grade is mitigated by significant student input into the process.

The Downtown Learning Center in Atlanta, Georgia, also uses contracts for both "in-building" and "out-of-building" study. Together the student and the instructor negotiate a contract which specifies the following information: the objectives of the course, the student's needs and wishes, and the instructor's ideas as to how those needs can best be met. All contracts are mutually renegotiable at any time. Some contracts are for an entire course; others are "mini-contracts" for one-quarter-hour credit.

The Rochester (New York) School Without Walls uses a dual evaluation system. Both the student and the teacher make periodic evaluations of the student's work; both evaluations become part of the student's academic record and can be used in whole or part as a transcript of academic progress. The student also keeps a log or journal. After spending four years in the program, the student appears before a certification committee consisting of two students, two staff members, and two community representatives. The panel reviews all the student's work, a student portfolio, all the cumulative evaluations, and then decides whether or not the student is eligible for graduation.

The Watertown (Massachusetts) Home Base School uses a three-part evaluation and reporting system, developed by a team of consultant–evaluators. One part is a monthly "interpersonal memo," a confidential statement written each month by the teacher of the course. According to the developers of the process, "It is confidential in order to create an atmosphere of honesty and safety that permits an appraisal of the work in a manner that is positive and personal" (Black and Patkin, 1973, p. 4). The second part is the final evaluation which includes the requirements for the course and an appraisal of the student's performance, along with a grade of pass or fail and comments concerning the student's strengths and weaknesses. The third part of the evaluation process is a transcript statement; the teacher of each course summarizes the specific requirements of the course and evaluates the student's work. The student's adviser summarizes the comments made by the individual teachers.

The Village School in Great Neck, New York, uses a portfolio system. The portfolio includes a written plan for the year, which the student develops early in September; in it the student outlines the goals for the year and the means by which those goals will be achieved. The portfolio also includes descriptive records of the student's educational experiences which the student compiles twice a year. Statements from people with whom the student has worked during the school year may also be included. Copies of the portfolio are available to the student, the parent, the adviser, and the director of secondary education.

The Walk-In School in Columbia, South Carolina, also uses a contract system, negotiated between the instructor and the student. A student may work on from one to six contracts at any time. When the student completes a contract, the instructor assigns a credit. According to school officials, there is no failure; either the student is rewarded a passing grade or the contract is renegotiated. A student may elect a letter grade of A, B, or C, and may contract for a letter grade when the initial contract is submitted.

The Southeast Free School in Minneapolis, Minnesota, has a unique procedure for determining when the student is eligible for graduation. A student may be certified for a diploma anytime after his or her sixteenth birthday. The procedure, according to school officials, is as follows:

1. Student and advisor agree six months in advance on target date for graduation.
2. Student and advisor, working with other staff, agree on a written contract for the final several months' work.
3. Contract covers minimum competence requirements not yet met, plus additional proficiency areas agreed to be appropriate for the student.
4. Student and advisor agree on student's Graduation Review Committee, to include two staff (other than advisor), one Free School parent (chosen from governing board), one secondary student, and one adult not formally related to Free School. Advisor serves as student's advocate before this committee.
5. Committee meets monthly with student and advisor.
6. At completion of contract the committee meets with student and advisor for final graduation interview ["Southeast Alternatives," 1974, p. 31].

Ryan High School in Omaha, Nebraska, uses an evaluation system which seems to be uniquely adapted to the school's individualized "packaged" learning. According to Virginia Roth, "At Ryan the students average twenty-five courses per year. At any one time they will be involved in four to six courses; and as they finish one, they will take the next course in sequence" (Roth, 1973, p. 17). Whenever a student finishes a course, he or she is given a credit slip from the teacher–consultant with whom the student has been working. The credit slip indicates which course was finished, the credits earned, and which course will next be started. The credit slip is completed in duplicate, with the original going to the learner to take home and the carbon to a department clerk who transfers the information to a profile card. The profile card is a comprehensive record of all the courses completed in that department by the individual student. Once every three weeks a clerk from the office gets the cards from each department and transfers the information to the student's permanent record.

What generalizations can be drawn from these and other systems reported in the literature and by the schools themselves? There seem to be several tentative conclusions that can be drawn:

1. The evaluation process in alternative schools emphasizes self-evaluation. The student is seen as the primary locus of the evaluation process.

2. The evaluation process is often a cooperative one. Student and teacher work together on the process.

3. Some kind of explicit contract is made between student and teacher. The contract usually spells out a goal, the methods to be used, and the evaluation process desired.

4. The student is given an option about the symbol used in the recording and reporting processes. Although many alternative schools are using "pass-fail" or "credit–no credit" systems, most still hang on to a letter grade option for students who want it.

Success of New Evaluation Schemes

How have new approaches to evaluation succeeded? Since we lack any systematic data, it is difficult to make a general judgment. There are, however, some beginning findings which at least give us some sense about success and problems.

To begin with, colleges have reported mixed reactions to the transcripts and evaluations from alternative schools. In general, the colleges seem to express a positive attitude about alternative programs and new forms of evaluations. A survey by the Center for Grading Alternatives of 2,000 colleges indicated that 77 percent indicated a willingness to accept students from schools experimenting with grading systems (Bellanca and Kirschenbaum, 1973). One director of admissions seemed to be speaking for many directors when he said, "We may be in a damn mess . . . but alternative education is going in the right direction" (Black and Patkin, 1973, p. 2).

Yet there have also been rumblings of discontent from some of the college people. The same study by Black and Patkin reported such comments as these from the admissions officers contacted: "I get piles of evaluations impossible to comprehend. . . . I don't know who is making these comments, and all they say is how great the kid is. How can one possibly exercise fair judgment without substantial information of a student's performance and skills?" Another added: "Alternate school transcripts are all alike . . . do not offer enough information to compare these students with those having conventional records" (Black and Patkin, 1973, p. 2).

These critical reactions were echoed in the evaluation of the Parkway transcripts performed by the Organization for Social and Technical Innovation:

> Many colleges complain at being sent Parkway folders instead of a transcript. Another result is that one student is indistinguishable from another on the basis of the bland prose descriptions. Only after reading fifteen evaluations on one student did we come across the following comment from an institutional teacher: "What else is there to say about X that hasn't been said before? He is a thoroughly obnoxious young man who . . ." And it went on to make some constructive comments. Nothing that we had read until then suggested the young man had any personality whatsoever ["Philadelphia's Parkway Program," 1972, p. 61].

When asked about their specific criticisms of alternative school transcripts, the college admissions officers surveyed mentioned the following:

> Incomplete transcripts in which only the years in the alternative school are included.
>
> Different types of transcripts for students from the same alternative school.
>
> Missing data such as dates and duration of courses and other pertinent information regarding academic performance.
>
> Unnecessary bulk, pages of unexplained information (Black and Patkin, 1973, p. 3).

From within the alternative schools themselves, the picture is similarly mixed. First, the author's own observations and numerous discussions with alternative school teachers and students indicate that the elimination of competitively based grading systems seems to improve the climate of learning. Teachers and students alike talk about such positive factors as "less anxiety and worry," "people now learn for learning's sake, not for the sake of the grading," and "there is no more cheating going on now." These personal observations are supported by Howard Kirschenbaum, director of the Center for Grading Alternatives, who has spoken with hundreds of teachers who have had success with alternative grading systems (Telephone conversation with author).

However, there are also problems inside the school. When the members of the staff of Concept I in Beachwood, Ohio, evaluated their own procedures, they gave this candid assessment:

> Student evaluation procedures and credit assignments are other areas in which changes have been made in an effort to avoid problems. After an attempt to utilize a modified contract system for evaluation purposes failed in the first year of Concept I, teachers had to resort to single year-end grades and credit negotiation. Although written forms, letter grades, and credit negotiations have always existed, dissatisfaction with various aspects of all of them has always been apparent [Kincaid, 1974, p. 48].

And at alternative school conferences, teachers have candidly admitted that evaluation continues to be a problem—too much time, too many forms, too much inefficiency, too much information.

New grading systems can probably work only if some systematic attention is given to developing a comprehensive evaluation process.

Improving Evaluation Processes

The author believes that all schools, conventional and alternative, should develop a comprehensive plan for evaluation that takes a fresh look at all aspects of the evaluation process. One difficulty with some of the new alternatives to grading is that they have focused on just the symbol used in the reporting stage, without considering new approaches to other phases. So the concern here is not simply with finding a better symbol system, but with finding ways to improve all phases of the process. Such a comprehensive revision, he believes, should include six separate stages of evaluation which he calls diagnosing, giving feedback, judging, grading, recording, and reporting. Let us examine each of these.

Diagnosing

Diagnosing is that stage in the evaluation process that comes at the beginning of the unit or course of study. It represents the attempt to find out where the learner is before the learning begins. A good diagnosis probes to try to find answers to these questions:

1. Does the learner have sufficient skills and knowledge to begin this unit?

2. How much of the unit does the learner already know?

3. What is the learner's preferred style of learning? Will he or she do better with more or less teacher direction, with self-paced or teacher-paced instruction, with an inductive or deductive process?

4. Which methods and materials of learning can the student use most profitably?

5. Which recurring problems in previous learning continue to be present and will affect learning?

Several methods can be used to effect a diagnostic evaluation. There are standardized diagnostic and achievement tests which can be used at the beginning of the year. The teacher can make up a pretest. The teacher can use an alternative form of the final summative evaluation. Regardless of the type of test used, the items included should be relatively easy. Benjamin Bloom and his co-authors recommend that a good diagnostic test should include a large number of easy items, with 65 percent difficulty or higher (Bloom, Hastings, and Madaus, 1971, p. 92). Even if tests are not used, classroom teachers can still be taught how to observe student behavior and performance in the classroom, using a simple checklist as a guide. Or a brief discussion at the opening of class can enable the teacher to probe for weaknesses and problems.

When should the teacher and the school diagnose? Three times seem especially important. First, when the student is enrolled in the alternative school or program, the teaching staff should arrange for a diagnostic interview in which the teacher, a counselor, the student, and the parent explore the student's past performance, his or her goals, the preferences for teachers and for ways to learn, and past record of academic problems and successes. Such a diagnostic session will help the teacher and counselor assist the student in making wise selections of courses and teachers. A second important stage for diagnosis is at the start of the course, when the teacher can use a standardized or teacher-made test to determine the student's existing level of knowledge and readiness for that subject.

Finally, the beginning of a unit of study requires careful diagnosis for readiness. In fact, every self-instructional system requires some type of pre-assessment before the learner begins the unit. To simplify the pre-assessment task for unmotivated students in an alternative career school, the author has developed and used effectively a two-part pre-assessment which includes a statement of "the skills you will need to complete this unit," and the suggestion, "If you think you already know all or part of this material, try the post-test at the end and check your answers."

Giving Feedback

The term "giving feedback" is used to identify a type of formative evaluation, a process by which the learner receives continuous information about his or her performance and achievement. While all teachers typically give some kind of feedback during class discussion and recitation, several mistakes are made in both alternative and conventional classrooms during the usual feedback process. First, the typical recitation actively involves a relatively small number of students. Second, the teacher often calls upon the student who has raised a hand, thereby giving feedback of an active sort only to the compulsive student who has a quick answer or the alert student who has the right answer. Finally, too many teachers respond positively even to answers that are wrong because they fear offending the student. If it is to help in the learning process, feedback must be negative as well as positive. Since feedback is a type of reinforcement, we strengthen undesirable behaviors if we respond to them with approval.

The feedback stage of the evaluation process can be improved in several ways. First, feedback should be specific, giving the learner information about strengths and weaknesses and suggesting how deficiencies might be remedied. Second, feedback should be provided to the entire class, not a selected few. A brief self-checking oral or written quiz can involve everyone and consume only a few minutes in each lesson. Also, others besides the classroom teacher should participate in giving the student feedback about his or her performance. Outside experts, other students, parents, and volunteers from the community can be brought in to give the student direct and immediate feedback. In this way the classroom teacher does not become the sole source of judgment and feedback.

Finally, wherever possible, we should help the learner derive his or her own feedback without our interposing ourselves in the feedback loop. This means that we should probably make more use of self-checking exercises, audio and video tapes of a student's performance, and models that can be used for self-discrimination.

Feedback should also be a two-way process, one in which the student is able to let the teacher know how he or she is succeeding. For this reason, we recommend that all classes end with some type of session in which the teacher asks the students to share orally their perceptions of their own and each other's performance and also to give the teacher honest feedback about the teacher's performance. From time to time the teacher should vary the oral feedback sessions with a short questionnaire, with just a few simple items like these:

The thing I liked best about this class was ———————— .
The thing I liked least about this class was ———————— .
In general, I thought this particular class was ——————— .

In this manner, students can begin to realize that feedback is necessary for all learning, even that of the teacher's.

Judging

The next stage in the evaluation process is judging, a term used here for the periodic summative evaluation. This evaluation establishes whether or not the student's performance meets some set of criteria or some standards of achievement. It comes at the end of a unit or of a significant learning experience. Despite the resistance of students to summative evaluation, some type is probably useful in letting the learner know how much has been accomplished, in showing the learner how to proceed next, in helping the teacher assess his or her teaching, and in giving the school information about its program. Finally, the results of the summative evaluation or judging are useful in making some final determination about grading and reporting. (These stages are discussed below.)

The summative evaluation can be fairest and most helpful to the student if he or she has been involved in determining in advance the objectives of the learning experience, or has at least been clearly informed about the objectives before the unit begins. It is here that the contract between student and teacher is most helpful, even though schools report difficulty in implementing the contract idea. If a contract is used, the student should state the objectives of the project or unit, indicate how those objectives will be attained, suggest how they will be measured, indicate what level of performance will be deemed satisfactory, identify what resources will be needed, and estimate how much time will probably be required. Whether or not an explicit contract is used, these matters should still be clear in advance to both learner and teacher. And any contract, explicit or implicit, should, of course, provide for and even facilitate the unplanned and unpredicted learning that is perhaps the most exciting and meaningful.

Once the contract has been completed or the student has finished the unit, the student and the teacher should cooperate in the summative assessment or judging. Typically, of course, this will be done with a written test, which samples all of the objectives in the unit so as to provide a fair assessment of mastery. But the summative evaluation does not have to be a written test; it can be an oral test, a demonstration, or the production of some unique creation. It also makes sense for people other than the teacher to perform the summative testing, if at all possible; in this way, the teacher is perceived as a helper, not as a judge.

At any rate, regardless of whether or not an outside evaluator is brought in, the judging process can be most effective if three guidelines are followed. First, the judging should yield specific information to the student about what has been learned and what has not been learned, what mistakes were made and how they can be improved, what problems were revealed and how they can be remedied. The judging process should be as analytical as possible so that the student finishes with rather precise knowledge about achievements and deficiencies.

Second, the teacher should analyze the data from the judging to assess the effectiveness of the learning material and the instruction. The teacher can simply return a test and ask the students to raise their hands if they had a particular item wrong. Such a simple item analysis will help the teacher improve the test and identify possible weak spots in a text or in teaching technique.

Finally, and perhaps most importantly, we should teach the student the skills of self-evaluation. The goal is to help the student develop into an autonomous learner who does not need someone else to act as judge, but who can make a fair and somewhat objective assessment of his or her own performance. This means that part of each course should involve some instruction in self-assessment: what criteria are important in this field of knowledge; how can one tell if a given approach or performance is better than another; what are the hallmarks of a good poem, a good essay, a good geometry proof, a good chemistry experiment?

Grading

Grading is the process whereby some symbol (such as a letter, number, or word) is assigned to the results of evaluation.

The teacher can evaluate without grading; in fact, it probably is a useful practice to give the student very specific evaluations without assigning a grade, but the teacher should not grade without evaluation. What symbols should be used? The author has already indicated that he thinks too much is made of the symbol itself, but he agrees that the matter can be a problem. His recommendation is to develop two simple symbol systems:

A, B, C, D, F
Credit   (No Credit)

The first is the traditional letter grade system so widely used and understood (albeit misinterpreted often). In the second, if the student does satisfactory work in a course, the word "credit" appears on the official record; if the course is not completed or the work is not satisfactory, no entry appears. The author prefers the "credit–(no credit)" system to "pass-fail," since he feels that the term "fail" has harmful connotations, and he clearly rejects refinements of the pass-fail system such as high pass, low pass, or pass with merit.

Once we have agreed about the symbol system or systems to be used, we should make the options and the unique advantages and disadvantages of each clear to the student. Give the student a choice here, and if he or she feels a clear grade is needed or preferred, that should be available. Despite all their obvious and oft-noted drawbacks, letter grades have some elements in their favor. They seem to be the best predictor of success in college; they are most generally understood; and they help large universities make some quick assessment of academic achievement. Students who eschew letter grades should realize that a long list of "pass-fail" or "credit–(no credit)" entries on a transcript make some admissions officers give more weight to College Board scores; at least, the author's survey of admissions officers revealed that.

Whenever possible, the student should be involved in the judging process, as an important part of the learning process. The best situation from the author's point of view is one in which the teacher helps the student make some objective assessment of final achievement. To that end he has developed a simple form which has worked successfully in structuring this cooperative evaluation process. (See Figure 2.)

Recording

Recording is the practice of noting in writing all the important evidence of student achievement. The recording process is the means by which the official record is developed. In most schools the teacher does the recording and does so only at stated intervals, such as report periods. And often the recording is the amassing of negative evidence. Alternative schools—and conventional schools as well—should change that. First, little is achieved by adding negative information to the student's official record. For this reason it probably would be useful to include in the school's record only passing grades or notations of credit. If the student does not get credit for a course, there is no need to record that. If a counselor or disciplinarian wishes, he or she may keep an informal or unofficial record of school problems, but such a record should be destroyed at the end of each year. The official record needs to include only objective data, such as number of days absent, courses taken and passed, and birth date. The schools should not participate in the national mania for dossier building.

The student's official folder should be open to everyone for the purpose of adding positive information. The student should be encouraged to add to his or her own folder very specific information about community involvement, independent learning, school activities, and other special accomplishments, especially those of a creative sort. The folder should be open, with no confidential records that contain information someone should not see.

Reporting

Reporting is the process of sharing information about the student's achievement with other people and institutions. Here we need to differentiate between audiences, for they have quite different needs. We should report frequently to parents, espe-

Figure 2

ALTERNATIVE SCHOOLS PROJECT

Subject Achievement Record

Name of Student _____ East _____ West _____

Name and Address of Parents _____

_____

Subject _____ Subject Teacher _____ Cycle _____

Grading System Preferred for Official Record: _____

Objectives of Course: The student will:

1. _____

2. _____

3. _____

4. _____

5. _____

6. _____

7. _____

8. _____

9. _____

10. _____

Student Self-Evaluation of Achievement	*Teacher Evaluation of Achievement*
I feel I have achieved in the following ways:	I feel that the student has achieved in the following ways:
I feel I have not achieved in these ways:	I feel that the student has not achieved in these ways:
I think I have earned the grade _____	In my view the student has earned the grade _____
(Add any other comments on back)	(Add any other comments on back)

cially when there is a noteworthy achievement or some important problem. Too often we equate the reporting stage with some periodic and usually negative judging. With parents, especially, we should report frequently, informally, and directly. And any reporting to parents should be as particular as possible, noting specific deficiencies or strengths and eschewing educational jargon. Reporting to parents should also invite a two-way flow of ideas; the teacher can simply ask the parent, "What feelings do you have about the school or this course?"

Reporting to colleges, as noted earlier, has caused alternative schools some problems, but the author feels these problems can be eliminated. He has several recommendations.

First, the student should cooperate in preparing the transcript, although the official and final version should be approved by school officials. However, the student should feel that the careful preparation of the final transcript is his or her responsibility. Second, the staff should be thoroughly briefed about the purpose of the transcript: to report to the college the most reliable and objective assessment of the student's total performance, both in the alternative school and in the conventional school. While teachers should try to help the student put the best foot forward, no purpose is served if the student's achievement is so inflated that he or she is accepted in a college where standards are too high.

As to the form of the record sent to the colleges, the procedure that will be most helpful to the student will be to use a standard transcript form, one that can be readily understood by admissions people, supplementing that transcript with only two items. The first item should be a one-page description of the alternative school or program, noting its unique characteristics in the most favorable light. The second item should be a one- to two-page summary of the student's unique accomplishments as culled from the folder by the student and approved by the counselor or teacher. This summary might include pertinent teacher comments, records of important community involvement or part-time work, notes of any important creative work, and evaluations by community adults who have worked with the student.

A System for Implementation

Such a comprehensive system can be implemented in any school without undue difficulty. First, the student's official folder is kept in the office, where it is easily accessible to the student, counselor, teacher, or anyone else who wants to add to it. The student is encouraged to add to the folder frequently, dropping in brief reports of significant achievements. The folder should stay in the office, however, since it will contain the completed evaluations.

Second, the staff develops a diagnostic form which is used at the start of the year or at the beginning of any course. This diagnostic form should also be open to the student; in fact, the student should be encouraged to add information to the form, noting special aptitudes or favorite methods of learning. The diagnostic form should be kept in the student's folder, with copies made for each teacher who works with the student.

At the start of a marking period or major unit of study or significant independent study project, the student completes a contract for each course, specifying the objectives (worked out cooperatively with the teacher), the means of reaching those objectives, the time required, the method of evaluation, the level of satisfactory performance, and the resources needed. The contract can be modified at any time by mutual agreement. Schools that do not wish to use an explicit contract might consider using some form similar to the one shown in Figure 2; the top half of the form can be completed by the student at the beginning of the marking period; the bottom half, at the end.

Periodically, the classroom teacher telephones or writes to the parents if special problems develop or if special achievement is noted. In some schools teachers are required to do this systematically once a month for each student; a brief note or a five-minute telephone call is usually considered sufficient. The school may wish to develop some interim reporting form which the teacher can check and mail. The important point is to build in a process for frequent communication.

During the last week of the marking period, the student completes the self-evaluation, using a portion of the contract or a form similar to the one shown in Figure 2. The student then confers with the teacher about the judgment, with the teacher completing the "teacher-evaluation" part of the form or contract. In case of any disagreement, the teacher and student should be encouraged to work out a compromise, but the school should make it clear that if none can be reached, the teacher's judgment will prevail.

The classroom teacher then forwards the form to the counselor–teacher. The counselor–teacher confers with the parents by telephone or in person and writes a summary of the student's overall achievement. If the counselor–teacher prefers, he or she may simply copy all the individual reports and mail them to the parents. The originals of the forms are filed in the student's official folder.

At the end of the year, or whenever necessary, the counselor–teacher meets with the student to compile the official transcript, using as input all the forms plus other available data. The student and the counselor–teacher decide together which teacher comments should go in the official record.

Each school may wish to develop its own evaluation system. The author's system can, of course, be improved, but he would suggest that all systems should meet these criteria:

1. There is continuous diagnosis before instruction.
2. Feedback is continuous and is two-way.
3. Some type of contract or statement of mutually agreed-on objectives is used.
4. The student has an option about the symbol system used for grading.
5. The student plays an active part in the judging (or summative evaluation) and in the grading.
6. The recording process results in an open and positive cumulative record of achievement.
7. Parents are contacted at least once a month.
8. Colleges receive a transcript which contains full information easily understood and evaluated.

Any system which meets those criteria will be a vast improvement over the present system or over solutions developed by schools which are simply tinkering with the symbols.

References

Barr, A. S., et al. *Wisconsin Studies of the Measurement and Prediction of Teacher Effectiveness*. Madison, Wisconsin: Dembar Publications, 1961.

Bellanca, James, and Howard Kirschenbaum (eds.). *College Guide for Experimenting High Schools*. Upper Jay, New York: Center for Grading Alternatives, 1973.

Billett, Roy O. "Provisions for Individual Differences, Marking, and Promotions." U.S. Office of Education Bulletin 1932, No. 17, National Survey of Secondary Education Monograph No. 13, Government Printing Office, 1933.

Black, Sam, and Judith Patkin. "Evaluation Report: Student Evaluation and Transcript Problems," Watertown, Massachusetts: Watertown School District, April 1973.

Bloom, Benjamin S., J. Thomas Hastings, and George F. Madaus. *Handbook on Formative and Summative Evaluation of Student Learning*. New York: McGraw-Hill, 1971.

Divoky, Diane (ed.). *How Old Will You Be in 1984?* New York: Avon Books, 1969.

Hoyt, Daniel P. *The Relationship Between College Grades and Adult Achievement: A Review of the Literature*. ACT Research Reports, No. 7, September 1965.

Johnson, Franklin W. "A Study of High School Grades," *School Review*, 19 (1911) pp. 13–24.

Kincaid, Lynda. "Beachwood City Schools: The Concept I Program," in *Alternative Programs in Greater Cleveland Public High Schools*, edited by Sally H. Wertheim. Cleveland: Martha Holden Jennings Foundation, 1974.

Kirschenbaum, Howard, Sidney B. Simon, and Rodney W. Napier. *Wad-ja-get? The Grading Game in American Education*. New York: Hart Publishing Company, 1971.

Martinez, Inez. "The Degrading System," in *Critical Teaching: Elegies to the Multiversity or Clarion for Carrion*, Teaching Assistant Association, University of Wisconsin, 1968, pp. 4–6.

Pallett, J. B. "Definition and Prediction of Success in the Business World," Unpublished doctoral dissertation, University of Iowa, 1965.

"Philadelphia's Parkway Program: An Evaluation," Newton, Massachusetts: Organization for Social Technological Innovation, 1972.

Postman, Neil, and Charles Weingartner. *The Soft Revolution*. New York: Dell, 1971.

Roth, Virginia. "A Model for an Alternative High School," Austin, Texas: Austin Writers Group, 1973.

Rugg, Harold O. "Teachers' Marks and the Reconstruction of the Marking System," *Elementary School Journal*, 18 (1918), pp. 701–719.

Shurtleff, Ray F. "Administrative Problems: Cambridge Pilot School," *National Association Secondary School Principals Bulletin*, September 1973, pp. 76–82.

Singer, J. E. "The Use of Manipulative Strategies: Machiavellianism and Attractiveness," *Sociometry*, 27, (1964), pp. 128–150.

"Southeast Alternatives," Minneapolis, Minnesota: Minneapolis Public Schools, 1974.

CHAPTER NINE

Decision Making

Many students and teachers report that one of the main reasons they opt for alternative schools and programs is a determination to assume more control over their own lives, to have an active voice in the shaping of that community called school. And it may well be that one of the most significant characteristics of alternative schools and programs is not their curriculum or their method of instruction but their governance, their way of sharing power and making decisions. Given that importance, then, it seems essential to examine in detail the matters of governance and decision making in alternative schools. This chapter, then, discusses briefly some criteria for evaluating decision-making structures, reviews the processes used by conventional schools in light of those criteria, examines the experience of alternative schools in trying to find some better structures, and concludes with some recommendations based upon that experience.

Criteria for Decision-Making Structures

What elements constitute good decision making? The following criteria are suggested for consideration.

First, the decision-making process should be effective. The organization is concerned with its own survival, and the decisions made should ensure its effective survival, not hasten its destruction. Bad decisions, democratically made, are still bad decisions.

Second, the decision-making process should be efficient. The essential business of the school is helping young people become more competent, not providing a forum for the discussion of personal and institutional problems. If any group of students and staff members spends inordinate amounts of time discussing, debating, and deciding, then energies become depleted, time is dissipated, and the business of learning is put aside.

Third, the decision-making process should be honest and open. This standard has many important implications. There should be no covert manipulation of other people in order to secure one's ends. There should be no deceit about the amount of real power and influence possessed by individuals and groups. And all decisions should be arrived at in open meetings in which all involved have full access to all data.

Fourth, the decision-making process should be democratic. That's a slippery term. It is used here in this sense: those affected by a decision are able to express their ideas openly about that decision and have some appropriate means of influencing that decision.

Fifth, the decision-making process should be rational. While there is always room for intuition and the creative flight of fancy, it is more likely that the decision will be a good one if it has been arrived at through rational processes, in which relevant data have been assembled and all the alternatives carefully examined.

Finally, the decision-making process should be unifying, not divisive. While it is impossible to make any decision that will please all participants, it makes good sense to avoid any major decision that will alienate a goodly portion of the constituents and result in destructive controversy.

Obviously, these criteria develop out of some deeply held values, which perhaps might best be explicated here. The author prefers democracy to autocracy and believes that people learn as they live. Those who live in a community that operates democratically are more likely to internalize democratic values and ways of being. The author values freedom for each individual, within the constraints of the rights of others. And he believes that students have the full rights of all citizens. He values reasonable boundaries and limits that define the territories of the self and the group, and believes that those limits and boundaries are best set by those who are part of that community. He values diversity of belief and considers it essential for the school to provide a forum where all ideas can be heard and all proposals objectively considered. And the author obviously values the survival of good schools. He believes that that survival can best come about if all schools develop effective and democratic methods of governance.

Decision Making in Conventional Schools

Because they are large organizations and part of bureaucratic systems, most conventional schools are operated on principles of benign despotism. A school board of lay adults makes basic policy, influenced primarily by militant teacher groups bargaining for salaries and angry taxpayers demanding budget cuts. A superintendent of schools acts as the school board's chief executive, managing the system and seeing to it that policies are carried out by subordinates. The superintendent delegates authority to a building principal, who becomes the chief decision maker in that school. The principal confers with the faculty in faculty meetings and meets with a parent advisory group or a parent–teacher association, but for the most part, the decisions are made unilaterally by the principal and carried out by the staff. A student council, composed primarily of college-aspiring middle-class youth, holds meetings, arranges for dances, carries out fund-raising activities, and occasionally passes a resolution suggesting that a new idea be considered. While this description cannot apply to all schools and the way they are governed, it is generally accurate, based upon visits to hundreds of schools and discussions with numerous school administrators, students, and teachers.

How does such a system rate according to the criteria proposed above? To begin with, the system is more or less effective. At least it localizes accountability. If the superintendent or principal consistently makes poor decisions, ways are found to remove him. The superintendent is dismissed, and the principal is transferred. Either way, the school as an organization survives. The system is also effective because it tends to be rational. Principals and superintendents have learned to be more or less orderly in their decision-making processes. And the system is efficient. Faculty meetings tend to be brief, and decisions are made with little delay. So the autocratic process used in most conventional schools is succeeding within its own lights. And its success probably ensures its continuation, as long as students and teachers remain relatively passive.

On two important grounds, however, the system is seriously at fault. First, it tends to be dishonest. As has been pointed out in another work (Glatthorn, 1968), the decision-making process used in most schools is essentially dishonest and closed. People are often manipulated. The principal pretends to the student council that it has power, when it truly is impotent. And most important decisions are made in closed board and faculty meetings, where those most affected are shut off even from knowledge of the process and the deliberations.

The other problem is that the system is inherently undemocratic. Students, most affected by the decisions made, have little opportunity to make their feelings known and almost no opportunity to affect those decisions. This impotence often results in the apathy that administrators most decry. As the author indicates elsewhere (Glatthorn, 1972), students who feel that they are impotent in the decision-making process will often manifest a pervasive apathy about all matters dealing with school. The other problem with the autocratically governed school is that it runs counter to the values and goals of this society, and the students living day by day in an autocratic environment come out poorly prepared to function democratically.

So some new systems of school governance are needed. The next section examines some experiments in decision making in alternative schools and assesses their success by the standards described above.

Decision Making in Alternative Schools

In an attempt to find more democratic methods, alternative schools have experimented with new ways of decision making. Although the staff of each school feels that the school's procedures are unique, alternative educators at a UNESCO-sponsored conference on decision making found that the approaches they developed had a surprising degree of commonality ("Decision Making in Alternative Schools," 1972).

What are these procedures and what can be learned from them? The author would like to tease out the lessons to be learned by putting together a composite picture of the worst practices of alternative school decision making. He would call it "Disaster at Utopian High," and it would go like this:

A group of warm, loving people decide to open an alternative school called Utopian High. They put together a weak governing board, just for window dressing, since they don't want "outsiders" interfering with their community. They decide to accept whoever wants to attend, since they are committed to an open community, and they don't worry too much about goal consensus, since they value diversity. They don't spend any time discussing how they will make decisions, since these things are best developed "organically." There is no need for a strong leader, since all power is to be distrusted. Since they believe so much in freedom and in youth, they do not bother setting any limits for behavior; all people are basically good and just need to be reminded of the rights of others. They assume that all students desperately want to be involved, and they anticipate the lively discussions at town meeting that will eventually develop organically into a consensus. So school opens. They give students all the privileges so long denied them—smoking, class cutting, open campus, and so on. For the first few weeks, town meeting is well attended, and people argue long and hard about all issues. Shortly, however, students stop attending town meeting, do not come to committee meetings, and begin to complain about the school. Things begin to fall apart, since no one is really in charge. The staff is exhausted. The school faces a crisis. At this juncture some one individual takes over and acts unilaterally, or else the staff members assume real control and make all the decisions at staff meeting. And the experiment in participatory democracy has failed.

While such a depressing picture is fortunately not one that would be found in its totality in any surviving alternative school, the author's experience and the experience of those who have written about these matters (see especially Cooper, 1973, Singleton, Boyer, and Dorsey, 1972, and "Student Involvement in Decision-Making," 1971) suggest that too many alternative schools make the serious errors embodied in that scenario of disaster. Perhaps a discussion of the most important errors will serve as a useful background for recommendations for improvement.

First, most alternative schools would profit from some sort of stable governing board with sufficient power to keep the school active and vital. As Bruce Cooper points out, if too much power is lodged in a staff, the high rate of teacher turnover in alternative schools means that there will be no stable group providing some sort of continuity for the school (Cooper, 1973). Jonathan Kozol makes the same point from a different perspective: the large prestigious board assembled for window dressing often turns out to be an obstacle to effective operation (Kozol, 1972b). A small board with real power carefully delineated will provide continuity without interfering unduly in the day-to-day operation of the school.

The second error is lack of goal consensus. While the author sympathizes and agrees in theory with those who value diversity and practice openness, he realizes the significant dangers in trying to be all things to all people. Fritz Mulhauser puts it this way:

> I would like to suggest a heresy: that it is time to give up the dream of making the melting pot work inside alternative schools, when it has not worked in any other segment of society. By melting pot, I mean the very basic idea that we ought to seek out and welcome every sort of student (and non-student) that now exists in public school. Not only does it seem to me this idea is hard to support on educational grounds, but when we add to it the usual additional goal in our schools of "creating community"—we are at the farthest limits of our ability. We just don't know how to bring it off, and I would like to suggest that the struggle is more enervating, exhausting, and perhaps damaging than the results justify [As quoted in "Decision Making in Alternative Schools," 1972, p. 68].

Cooper makes the point less dramatically but just as cogently: "Schools have little ability to contain tensions and pitched ideological battles, endangering member identification and intimacy. . . . Schools, therefore, with lower disparity among member goals . . . will stand a better chance of survival" (Cooper, 1973, pp. 503–504). The author thinks there is a way of escaping between the horns of this dilemma of diversity and commonality, as will be explained later.

The third mistake is a belief in some "organic" process and a distrust of something called structure. Such a mistake stems from a naïveté about organizations and individuals. Confusion develops organically; structures for orderly decision making do not. Researchers who studied the decision-making process at Metro High School in Chicago put it this way:

> Program initiators should establish an initial structure for governance that will reconcile the goals of institutional survival and development with the goal of involvement in decision-making rather than hoping one will "emerge." . . . To hope that structure will "emerge" from the community might be slightly simpler initially. However, since the types of structure that are almost always proposed have a history of failing, the long-range effect will almost certainly be alienation, exhaustion, and the drastic curtailment of participation when ineffective methods of decision-making pro-

mote crisis ["Student Involvement in Decision-Making," 1971, p. 56].

Robert Riordan speaks of that same need for structure:

> Alternative schools must realize that structure and discipline, far from being antithetical to their principles, are the prerequisites to building a viable alternative setting. For example, in the area of governance, people must work to develop listening and decision-making skills to accomplish the common goal of shared decision-making [Riordan, 1972, p. 42].

The fourth error is the distrust of power. While it is fashionable among certain utopian dreamers to dream of a society where all people are leaders and genuine consensus is easily achieved, the reality is otherwise. In any organization certain individuals hold power, in terms of the resources they command and the influence they wield. And for any organization to survive, this power must be used honestly and wisely by some individual chosen to be leader. Jonathan Kozol is almost vitriolic in his criticism of those who are afraid of power, criticizing those teachers who "reduce themselves to ethical and pedagogical neuters" (Kozol, 1972a, p. 51). He blames this weakness on a "fear of power" that

> places a premium on mediocrity, nonvital leadership, insipid character, and unremarkable life style. An organization, of whatever kind, that identifies real excellence or effectiveness with the terrifying risk of authoritarian manipulation will drive away all interesting and brilliant people and will establish in their stead norms of communal mediocrity [p. 53].

The next error is common to the adult who adulates the young: the belief that no limits are needed, since young people will naturally do what is right. Both the group and the individual, however, seem to profit when broad limits are clearly defined. First, the organization needs limits in a hostile world which venerates the law in order to ensure its survival; it also needs to reduce the level of conflict resulting from ill-defined limits and to protect itself against the encroachment of self-centered individuals. And Glorianne Wittes sees limits desirable from the students' point of view:

> Tension provokes participation in attempts to change the unpalatable situation. Institutional structures and constraints (provided they are not unduly repressive) may be more productive to teach citizenship skills to kids than an environment which, like a vacuum, poses no constraints to move against [As quoted in "Decision Making in Alternative Schools," 1972, p. 27].

One of the most significant errors is the assumption that all students desire to participate actively in the process of governance. The experience of those of us in alternative schools who have worked hard to achieve such involvement is that such a perception ignores a very important difference between instrumental and expressive concerns. As these terms were first used by Amitai Etzioni (1964), they describe two different functions of any organization: the instrumental realm of activity is related to the official functions of the organization; the expressive realm, to people's personal concerns. Now the experience of alternative schools is that students are deeply concerned about expressive matters, but not about instrumental concerns. Once the school has granted the students the privileges they want, they lose interest in influencing the decision-making process. The study of student involvement at Metro makes this observation:

> Coming from traditional schools, the major concern of Metro students was to gain autonomy in the expressive realm. Metro staff strongly encouraged this direction, and they considered freedom of movement, dress, expression, association, etc., fundamental to the program's design from the beginning. Thus, in the areas that students cared more about, there was no need for participation in decision-making to gain desired ends. The battle had already been won ["Student Involvement in Decision-Making," 1971, p. 10].

The instrumental concerns of the staff—curriculum, scheduling, materials and supplies, school organization—were simply not ones that students cared about.

Other mistakes add to the debacle. There is too much reliance on the town meeting as a decision-making process, with

issues quickly decided by a hasty vote of the bored and unin-
terested. There is a tired staff, untrained in governance and
rational decision making, spending many hours in unproduc-
tive wrangling and rhetorical infighting. And there is some
impulsive action by a teacher or group of teachers who has
gotten tired of inaction and delay.

And these mistakes mean that the alternative schools'
decision-making process is democratic and honest, but too
often inefficient, ineffective, and irrational. All these mistakes
can be avoided if the staff works out in advance structures for
decision making that will respond to the unique situation of the
alternative school.

Structures for Decision Making

What are those appropriate organizational structures? Every
alternative school develops its own decision-making groups
and its own nomenclature, but the following structures seem to
be most common and most functional.

The Board

Called variously the community board, board of trustees,
or board of directors, this group of individuals determines policy for the school. Even when the alternative school operates
within a public school system directed by an adult school
board, it will often have its own board making policies that
apply only to the alternative school. Typically, board members
are elected, not appointed; they operate with their own bylaws
and meet periodically to conduct official business. In many
alternative schools board members are elected from the community to ensure community control. In others the board includes representatives elected from among students, teachers,
parents, and other constituent groups. (In alternative schools
affiliated with public school systems, district administrators
and/or school board members often have representation on the
alternative board.)

Jonathan Kozol, in his book *Free Schools* (1972b), wisely
points out the dangers of a large, prestigious board and advo-

cates instead either a small, benevolent dictatorship of the eight or ten core people in a school or a revolving board elected by those who are studying and teaching in the school. His point seems well taken. And both studies of decision making in alternative schools by the Center for New Schools recommend some type of governing board. ("Student Involvement in Decision-Making," 1971, and "Decision Making in Alternative Schools," 1972.) Large political boards composed of conflicting interest groups often become locked in power struggles. But small boards, drawn from the school's constituencies and sharing common goals, seem to be effective stabilizing forces for otherwise unstable schools.

The Director

In almost every successful alternative school there is some designated leader called director or head teacher. Several alternative schools have tried other leadership patterns. Some use a two-man team (an "inside man" and "outside man"); some use a small group of "managers"; and others seem to thrive for a while on anarchy. But almost all discover somewhat painfully that there has to be one person in charge, who is not afraid to use legitimate power.

Two other lessons have been learned from alternative school experience about leadership. The first is that the leader must be an integral part of the community, spending full time in that school. Schools that have operated with a part-time director, dividing his or her time between two or three units, or with a remote leader, trying to administer from the main building, have found that such schemes just don't work. Even in small alternative schools it is better to have a teacher on site devote part of his or her time to unit leadership than to have a part-time director run in and out one or two days a week or to have someone out of touch with the unit try to govern it.

The other lesson is that the leader will be more effective if he or she has been chosen by the staff and if there is a specific term for his appointment. Often a skillful leader appointed by some outside authority (such as a district superintendent) can successfully enlist staff support from the outset and in effect function as one of the staff, but the chances for harmonious relationships seem greater if the staff has had an active part in the selection of their director. And a limited term of office, perhaps for two or three years, is one way of guaranteeing self-renewal through leadership change. Even a successful leader should surrender his or her position, simply to ensure that a fresh perspective is brought to the school.

The Primary Group

Somewhat analogous to the homeroom in the conventional school, the primary group (sometimes called the tutorial, the counseling group, the family, or the tribe) is the basic organizational unit for the school. Like the homeroom, the group is the locus for such routine administrative business as checking attendance and disseminating information. But in the alternative setting, it is different from the typical homeroom in quite significant ways.

First, it meets on a regularly scheduled basis for an hour or two each week. Second, it is a structure where much group guidance takes place. Third, it becomes a significant channel for home–school communication. Also, it becomes the primary group where the students make friends and build social relationships. And finally, it plays a key part, as we shall see, in the decision-making process.

Clearly, such an organizational structure as the primary group can discharge all these important functions successfully only if optimal conditions prevail. Teachers should get explicit training in group processes to help them weld a collection of individuals into a cohesive group. The groups should probably be as heterogeneous as possible, reflecting the composition of the entire school. Through such heterogeneous core groups, the staff can probably accomplish a great deal in breaking down the stratification that inevitably develops even in small schools. Finally, the groups should meet on a regularly scheduled basis, perhaps for an hour twice a week—enough time to get important tasks done but not so much that boredom ensues.

The Town Meeting

Sometimes called the forum, the community meeting, or the assembly, the town meeting is the gathering of the entire school community. In some alternative schools the town meeting is held on a regular schedule, such as the first hour every Monday morning; in others it is held only when there is an important reason for it.

Whether scheduled or unscheduled, the town meeting plays an important part in the life of the community. It is an effective means for disseminating information quickly to a large group. It can be a place where students can have useful experience in leading and directing a large group. It can be the structure through which enthusiasm is engendered and school cohesiveness is developed. And it can play a critical role in the decision-making process. (See Bremer and von Moschzisker, 1971, for a description of a town meeting in action.)

In many alternative schools, however, students will freely tell inquiring visitors that the town meeting is a waste of time. And even the sympathetic observer, seeing the mindless wrangling, the angry speech making, and the adolescent pontificating is inclined to agree. But these difficulties can be minimized with some simple precautions. Students and staff can develop some basic ground rules for the conduct of the meeting and the handling of business. Strong student leaders can be given special training to enable them to function more effectively with an audience of a hundred or more excited peers. And student and staff observers can take a few minutes at the end of each meeting to give the entire group some honest feedback about the processes used and the progress accomplished.

The Committees

No democratic society can exist without committees, and alternative schools are no exception. In fact, it seems at times that every student in an alternative school has his or her name on at least two committees. Some alternative schools operate with a large number of standing committees, usually in such areas as curriculum, building and grounds, community relations, budget, evaluation, sports and activities, transportation, governance and government, and scheduling. Other alternative schools have few or no standing committees but instead convene ad hoc task forces to address specific problems as they arise. "Anybody interested in improving the transportation situation come to the lounge at 2:30 today!"

Whether standing committees or ad hoc task forces, these committees, as they are found in alternative schools, are composed of staff and student volunteers, are often chaired by a student, not a teacher, and do much of the real work of school governance. In fact, often a few active committees in an alternative school are doing most of the dirty work that needs to be done.

The Staff Meeting

Much of the important day-to-day decision making takes place in staff meetings. In fact, a common complaint of alternative school teachers is that they spend more time in staff meetings than they do in classroom sessions. And a common complaint of students is that too many decisions affecting them are made in staff meetings.

Such a condition is easy to understand. In a small staff of strong-minded adults, opinions are likely to be vehemently expressed and feelings openly vented. With a staff that believes in participatory decision making, even trivial issues seem to warrant extended examination and debate. And with a staff that welcomes students at staff meetings as a manifestation of openness, the large size of the group often inhibits the efficient accomplishment of business.

But such situations can at least be ameliorated. The staff members themselves can decide that they will hold one required meeting each week for purposes of decision making, with time limits clearly set; others who want to gather to examine their psyches can do so as they please. An agenda can be developed cooperatively, with a time limit set for each item.

The person who adds an item to the agenda can be given the responsibility of leading discussion on that item. And some simple means of checking attitudes—such as an informal show of hands or a quick polling of all involved—can cut through the red tape of parliamentary procedure. And a government committee composed of teachers and students can check to be sure that staff meetings do not decide issues which more properly belong on a town meeting agenda.

So the names may vary, and the details of their operation may be dissimilar, but almost every alternative school develops the same basic organizational structures: a policy-making board, a leader, a staff, a meeting of the entire community, a primary group, and special committees.

Making the Structures Work

How can such organizational structures be made to function effectively in the decision-making process? Although there is no one pattern that is best for all schools, a distillation of the experience of successful schools suggests that procedures such as the following will work with an improved measure of effectiveness, efficiency, and rationality.

Goal Consensus Is Established

At the outset those planning the school and most committed to its success determine the kinds of students the school will serve and the school's general goals. In a sense this is the crucial period, when the planners determine the central mission of the school they will open. And they boldly announce to all interested what that mission will be: "We will be a tightly run school stressing basic skills." "We will be a free and open school developing creativity." "We will be a community learning how to live together." "We will be a career school stressing no-nonsense competency." In this way they move quickly toward goal consensus by inviting and welcoming only those to whom that central mission appeals.

Thus, we do not have to have alternative schools or programs that try to be all things to all people. We can have a
range of alternative schools and programs, each with its own
special mission, serving very diverse populations.

The Boundaries Are Set

All those who are to play a significant part in the school
—students, staff, and parents—meet at the opening of the
school to set the broad boundaries in which the school will
operate. By meeting in small work groups and then by considering together the recommendations of the several groups, the
community develops tentative answers to such basic questions
as the following:

1. What general processes should be used in making decisions? What authority will the board have? How much power
should the director have? What decisions will be made by the
staff? How will major decisions be made by the entire community? In what areas and in what ways can parents be involved?

2. What boundaries already exist for the school? What
federal directives, state laws, and local ordinances most critically affect the school? Is there some superordinate group
—such as a school board—to which we, as members of the
school, are responsible?

3. What basic ground rules do we need about people's
conduct and behavior? (Most alternative schools develop one
set of rules for students and teachers alike.) What stance should
we take on such problems as class cutting, drugs, smoking,
stealing, fighting, and vandalism?

4. By what processes and under what policies should we
deal with those who consistently violate the boundaries?
Under what conditions will we ask someone to leave the
school? (While some schools desire to be inclusive communities that never ask anyone to leave, most find it essential at
some point in time to exclude those whose conduct threatens
the existence and welfare of the community. And such a contract needs to be spelled out in advance.)

5. By what processes and how often should these bound-

aries be reviewed and revised? (Such a review is so essential that it must be planned and legitimized during this critical boundary-setting process.)

In this fashion, then, the entire school community develops the basic contract by which it will live.

The Board Organizes

With the basic contract developed, the board organizes itself for its business, developing its bylaws and electing its officers. Many of the early board policies will be developed simply by ratifying and codifying the major parts of the contract previously developed. But the board will also want to focus more specifically on personnel and fiscal matters that require more official action.

Problems Are Solved

With such preliminary groundwork accomplished, the school can now develop its basic problem-solving and decision-making process, which might go something like this:

1. A problem surfaces. In an open environment problems will readily come to the surface. Sometimes they might get first formal notice in a group meeting, sometimes in a committee meeting, sometimes in a class, or sometimes in a town meeting. Some problems are so small that they get solved at this stage by immediate action. Others are so trivial that they fade away without any action.

2. The problem is brought to the attention of the community. The more serious problems are presented in town meeting.

3. Someone in charge decides how the problem should be dealt with. Some problems require direct action by one individual. ("The toilets don't work." "Get a plumber.") Some can be dealt with on the spot by a quick polling of those present. ("We need more time for this town meeting." "How many feel we should extend our meeting time right now?") But major problems should not be acted on without further study. ("Our evaluation system needs improving." "Let's study it first.")

4. A group of interested people study the problem and get the necessary data. The director or the person in charge either refers the matter to a standing committee or creates a task force to study the problem. "All those interested in studying ways to improve our evaluation system meet with Warren tomorrow at 2:30 in the lounge. We'll expect a report within two weeks."

5. The task force presents its recommendations. For important and complex problems, where the recommendations themselves are likely to be complicated, it seems best to have the task force present its report in writing to the core groups. In the small-group settings, time can be taken to be sure that everyone understands what is being proposed, and everyone present can have an opportunity to respond and react. With major questions that will have a significant bearing on the life of the school, the task force will probably want to get feedback from these small groups before developing its final set of recommendations.

6. The recommendations are acted upon at town meeting. By this time, hopefully, everyone has had a chance to understand, review, and respond to the recommendations, so that the discussion at the town meeting should be focused and constructive. And in order to avoid the divisiveness that often results from a decision by majority vote, most alternative schools will take affirmative action only if two-thirds or three-fourths of those present in town meeting approve the recommendations.

Such a procedure need not be inflexibly followed, in alternative schools or in regular schools. But all effective decision-making procedures will probably involve some processes where the following steps are taken in sequence:

1. Once a problem has been identified, a decision is made about its importance.
2. For all important problems, data are gathered and alternatives are examined.
3. A specific set of proposals is developed to deal with the problem; these proposals are reviewed and discussed in

a small-group setting, where it is possible to ensure rational discussion and reasoned debate.

4. A final decision is made only when an overwhelming majority of the community is willing to support a position.

As perhaps can be seen, such a decision-making process can be time-consuming and complex. It would be more efficient to have all decisions made by the director. It would be more democratic to have all major decisions thrashed out in town meeting. But neither efficiency nor democracy alone is enough. We must instead develop some decision-making process, like the one described, that meets the following criteria:

1. It is efficient enough to keep the school functioning effectively without consuming too much time.

2. It is rational, examining all alternatives, gathering significant data for each option, predicting the consequences of all actions, and choosing logically that option most likely to bring about desired action.

3. It is effective, keeping the school alive and growing.

4. It is democratic, involving all those who will be affected by the decision.

5. It is open and honest. All who care about the issue have a chance to be heard; all sides are openly explored; and no action is taken in secret.

Any process that meets these criteria, regardless of the structures used, will be a good one for both alternative schools and conventional schools.

References

Bremer, John, and Michael von Moschzisker. *The School Without Walls: Philadelphia's Parkway Program*. New York: Holt, Rinehart, and Winston, 1971.

Cooper, Bruce. "Organizational Survival," *Education and Urban Society*, Vol. 5, No. 4 (August 1973), pp. 4–5.

"Decision Making in Alternative Schools: Report from a National Conference," Chicago: Center for New Schools, 1972.

Etzioni, Amitai. *Modern Organizations*. Englewood Cliffs, New Jersey: Prentice-Hall, 1964.

Glatthorn, Allan A. "The Principal and the Student Council." Washington, D.C.: National Association of Secondary School Principals, 1968.

Glatthorn, Allan A. "The Student As Person," *Theory into Practice*, Vol. 11, No. 1 (February 1972), pp. 17–21.

Kozol, Jonathan. "Free Schools," *Saturday Review*, March 4, 1972a.

Kozol, Jonathan. *Free Schools*. Boston: Houghton Mifflin, 1972b.

Riordan, Robert. *Alternative Schools in Action*. Bloomington, Indiana: Phi Delta Kappa Educational Foundation, 1972.

Singleton, Steven, David Boyer, and Paul Dorsey. "Xanadu: A Study of the Structure Crisis in an Alternative School," *Review of Educational Research*, Vol. 42, No. 4. pp. 525–531, 1972.

"Student Involvement in Decision-Making in an Alternative High School: A Preliminary Analysis," Chicago: Center for New Schools, 1971.

CHAPTER TEN

Places
and Spaces

One of the major contributions of the alternative school movement has been to force school staffs to reexamine the whole question of facilities and spaces for learning. Prior to the alternative school movement, the only questions school planners asked were, "Where should we build the school? How many rooms? How much money?" As a consequence, during the school-building boom of the sixties, the landscape was dotted with thousands of new cinder-block buildings, looking distressingly alike, costing millions of dollars; and now some ten years later several of those buildings stand half-empty. Hopefully, those mistakes of the sixties— which solved space problems by just building more schools— are a thing of the past, for the alternative school movement has shown us that more creative solutions are possible.

This chapter examines these creative solutions from three vantage points: What types of facilities are now being used in alternative schools? What have we learned from alternative school experience about the use of space? And how can these principles be applied in the planning of new buildings and the remodeling of old?

New Places for Schools

Once we begin with the assumption that it makes sense to bring students together in a common place for learning (an assumption, incidentally, that is being seriously challenged by Ivan Illich, 1971, John Holt, 1972, and others), we then need to ask about the nature of that space. And if we reject the idea that our requirements mandate a new school building, we can start to examine the host of options that are available. (An excellent survey of new uses of space by alternative schools can be found in "Places and Things for Experimental Schools," 1972.)

1. Capture space within the existing building. Perhaps the easiest solution is just to capture space within the regular building. Such a solution simply means the reallocation of existing space, with minimal expense and bother. Berkeley High School, for example, now houses three different experimental programs. Such reallocation is easiest in those modern schools—originally designed for team-teaching arrangements—where separate pods radiate from central facilities like libraries and cafeterias. When such sharing of a building takes place, it seems to work out best if there is a very clear delineation between the territory of the alternative school and that of the regular school; thus, if an entire floor or a separate wing or a special pod is reserved for the alternative, fewer conflicts over rule and territoriality seem to develop.

2. Remodel existing schools. An increasing number of old schools are becoming available for use. In some cases districts are building new schools, vacating the old building because it doesn't have the facilities required or isn't large enough to accommodate the increased population. In other cases the district discovers that enrollments are decreasing so significantly that it seems economical to vacate a building. In both situations the vacated building turns out to be quite suitable for an alternative school; such buildings of older vintage are often soundly constructed and can be remodeled without excessive costs to meet the needs of alternative programs. The Alternative East (Alternative Schools Project, suburban Philadelphia), for example, found that an abandoned elementary school made an excellent alternative facility without any remodeling. Students, in fact, who were used to very modern high school buildings, said enthusiastically that they thought the old granite schoolhouse had "a lot of great charm."

3. Old residential buildings. In older sections of city and suburb, it is often possible to find large residences that can be modified to accommodate alternative programs. The Shady Lane School in Pittsburgh, Pennsylvania, found that an abandoned mansion was ideally suited for their educational purposes. The main drawback—aside from troublesome zoning problems—is that these old houses were not built with modern fire codes in mind, and expensive fire escapes often have to be added. But the advantages make these buildings worth serious investigation: they are usually situated on well-landscaped grounds; the rooms are large enough for most classroom purposes; and there is a very obvious "homey" atmosphere that strongly appeals to counter-culture youth.

4. Available industrial space. Alternative schools are finding two types of industrial and commercial space usable for their purposes. In some suburban areas they are leasing space in newly developed industrial parks. While such space is often attractively designed and easily modified for school purposes, rental costs are sometimes prohibitively expensive. A much less expensive solution—at least initially—is to locate abandoned or underused commercial or industrial space and modify it to suit local needs. For such purposes factory lofts seem ideal: they provide expanses of open space that can readily be adapted for educational use. The examples of such "found space" are numerous among alternative schools: the Sea Pines Montessori School in Hilton Head Island, South Carolina, is located in a former souvenir shop on the edge of the ocean; the KLH Child Development Center in Cambridge, Massachusetts, uses an old refrigerator warehouse; the Community Learning Center in Washington, D.C., is located in an old supermarket; the Pennsylvania Advancement School in Philadelphia is an old factory loft.

5. Available institutional space. Every community has several churches and synagogues most of which have large religious schools standing empty during the week. And churches are almost always looking for additional revenue. As a consequence, many alternative schools have at least tem-

porarily taken up quarters in Sunday schools. The advantages of such quarters are obvious: they are designed as classrooms; they meet all building code and fire regulations; and they are usually available at quite reasonable rentals. But the drawbacks from the students' point of view are quite critical: the facilities typically have a hard institutional look, and since they are shared facilities, the students cannot make their own impact on them; and petty problems about bulletin boards, chairs, and blackboards make life complicated for the harried alternative school director.

6. Claimed space in new buildings. Since there is some new construction in suburban areas, it becomes quite feasible for alternative school planners to claim space while the school is in the planning stages. If a high-rise apartment building is being planned, it might be possible to secure reduced rentals by persuading the owners that a small alternative school located on the ground floor would be an attractive sales feature. Or if a new office complex is being planned, it might be possible to reserve some of the space for alternative school offices and a few classrooms.

7. Moving space. Since youth of the seventies seem to be a generation on wheels, some alternative schools use buses, campers, and even boats. The Alternative Schools Project in suburban Philadelphia, for example, leased a large Winnebago camper for a three-month period and made a series of trips to Washington, D.C. (to lobby for peace), to Webster Groves, Missouri (to make a documentary of suburban teen-agers), and to New England (to paint and visit art museums). The Omnibus School of Survival, centered in Sausalito, California, used an eighty-three-foot schooner for its school, making an extended trip to the Caribbean and back to San Francisco. While such mobile schools pose some obvious risks, their advantages in broadening the horizons of the young make them very attractive for alternative school purposes.

8. The "nowhere school." If we assume that education involves only experience and the assistance of some mature person to help the student process that experience, then we really

don't need a building at all. We simply need a network of people who can be identified as resources for learning. And the only space we need is an office for answering mail and making telephone calls. This approach, widely used in "universities without walls" in both England and the United States, has not been used too extensively at the secondary level here, probably because young people have such strong socialization needs and are really not too interested in a program of total independent study. However, during a prolonged teachers' strike, the Philadelphia school district mailed out correspondence lessons to its seniors and had limited success in keeping them caught up with their academic work. The promise of video casette libraries makes it even more likely that the "school" of the future might be a library of video tapes and a central office advising students, giving examinations, and awarding credits.

9. The "everywhere school." The "everywhere" school begins with a systematic analysis of a community's space resources: YMCA's, museums, churches and synagogues, community centers, swimming pools and athletic fields, art centers, libraries, parks, colleges and specialized schools, office buildings, shopping malls, hospitals and nursing homes, greenhouses, factories, filling stations, bowling alleys, country clubs, police and fire houses, and research institutes. The school's planners then decide which kind of learning can best take place in those various centers and analyze availability of space, possibilities of multiple use, transportation, and cost. They then put together a network of places that makes optimal use of space with minimal cost and inconvenience. One of the most ambitious of such plans is being produced under the aegis of the Lowell (Massachusetts) Model Cities Program. This old industrial city will be turned into a huge Human Development Center, an educational complex for all ages and all types of learning, reaching out and using all major resources of the city.

So in the alternative school experience, "school" has become something more than a cinder-block enclave of thirty-by-thirty-foot classrooms; school is any place where students and teachers can gather for learning.

Lessons About Space and People

What have we learned from our experience in alternative schools, in regular schools, and in the other spaces we live in? What insights have we gained about space and about people and about how these two interact? What do we know about learning and space requirements? This is not the place for an extended discourse about the environment and human psychology, but perhaps it would be helpful to extract from experience and the available research some basic principles that will surely affect how we make optimal use of space in human institutions.

After a few decades of architectural planning and a few years of alternative school experience, several lessons have become clear:

1. Territory is important. Man is space- and place-oriented. He fixes himself by the boundaries of place, as Edward Hall makes clear; he needs to feel that he occupies a special place of turf, one that he can claim for use by himself and his friends (Hall, 1966). And perhaps as we become more mobile as a people, moving about from motel to motel, from city to suburb, from ground to air, that special territory back home, familiar in its boundaries, markings, and features, will become even more important.

2. Space affects relationships. Careful studies have documented what most of us intuited: spatial arrangements strongly affect personal relationships. (See, for example, Goffman, 1971, and Lang, 1971.) People whose work and living spaces are close together develop close relationships and have higher frequencies of personal encounter; people whose working and living spaces are somewhat remote feel estranged and distant. If the principal's office is off in a separate wing, that spatial isolation will inevitably result in social and professional isolation.

3. Space requires clear definition to become "territory." Human beings have difficulty dealing with boundless space: give a man an open field and the first thing he will do is put up a fence. Space needs to be bounded and defined by visual markers before we can feel comfortable with it. Architects who built barnlike schools with only open space returned to their small offices and wondered why teachers and students reported being uncomfortable with the undefined space of the open school.

4. Clearly defined space and the visual and tactile aspects of that space affect mood, as Somer (1969) and others remind us. Hard chairs, hard desks, and hard floors help us settle down to serious business. Soft cushions in front of a fireplace invite relaxation and quiet talk. Soft earth and grass invite tumbling and falling. Trees with low-hanging branches are for swinging and sitting under. We need different kinds of space for our different moods.

5. Space should be single in type of use, multiple in types of users. We usually reverse this distinction in schools: we build seventy-five rooms, thirty by thirty feet, all furnished and painted exactly alike—for very different kinds of learning and being—and then limit their use to one type of user, the adolescent student. It makes sense instead to develop special spaces for very different kinds of use, and then make those spaces clearly available to all—students, teachers, and the larger community.

6. Human use determines material form. There's the old story of the landscape architect who opened the public park without paths. After six months of public use, he saw where the concrete walkways had to go—where the people had been walking for six months. People find their own directions, make their own patterns, and no planner can predict what those patterns will be. So it makes sense to leave space somewhat unfinished and only partially defined—and let the people finish the job in their own terms, according to their own real needs.

In a similar vein, what have we learned about the adolescent and his special needs for space? These things seem quite clear:

1. At times the adolescent wants to be alone. Despite his gregarious nature, there are periods of time when he wants total isolation, in what Aase Eriksen (1973) calls "private learning space." And one of the problems with almost all our schools is simply that there is no place to hide.

2. The adolescent spends much of his free time in cliques, a group of six to nine close friends. D. C. Dunphy (1963), among others, documents the importance of the clique for the adolescent. For all adolescents the clique structure is important, even though he may make ritual noises opposing cliques.

3. Cliques form crowds. Sociological analysis of adolescent interactions (see Coleman, 1961, for example) reveals that the other important social unit of the adolescent is the crowd—a group of perhaps twenty to thirty teen-agers—which is the primary unit of social life. Crowds are active on weekends in holding parties and dances; cliques are active during the week, talking over the previous gathering and planning the next one.

4. Oral activity is important for the adolescent. Gay G. Luce, in her summary of the research on physiological rhythms in man and animals, points out that most of us have a ninety-minute cycle of some type of oral activity—smoking, eating, drinking, chewing gum (Luce, 1971). Even casual observation of teen-agers indicates that this ninety-minute cycle is quite important; much crucial teen-age business is done over food, Cokes, and cigarettes.

5. The adolescent needs to leave his mark upon the environment. The graffiti covering the walls of schools and community buildings provide ample evidence of the adolescent's need to put his mark upon his place. He wants to change the space and the environment, for in changing it makes it his own.

Finally, what real lessons have we learned about the learning experience and the space it requires? Too often in school planning we have begun by identifying school subjects and ended with a laundry list—we need five English rooms, a home economics suite, an industrial arts shop, and so on. The other mistake is that we define space use by age groups and status, and thus effectively keep students and teachers from interacting except in the artificial classroom environment. If we begin instead with an analysis of what people will be doing in the place, where they want to learn together, we come up with quite different uses and types of space.

Here is a list of the things people seem to do when they come together to learn:

1. Sit and talk informally about a topic.
2. Sit alone and introspect.
3. Perform certain kinds of experiments under carefully controlled environmental conditions.
4. Use tools, machines, and materials to fashion their own products.
5. Sit together in large groups to listen to a speaker, see a film, or watch a performance.
6. Perform gross physical movements—dance, throw balls, jump, run.
7. Sit still for intensive study of a film, cassette, or book.
8. Eat, smoke, drink, and talk together with close friends.
9. Use communications media—phone, typewriter, xerox, visuals—to communicate with large groups.
10. Play active sports—baseball, softball, soccer—throw frisbees.
11. Lie down and relax or take a nap.
12. Use toilet and washbasin.
13. Take care of official business—answer correspondence, answer and make telephone calls, file official records.

Taken together, these general findings about space, youth, and learning can provide some useful guidelines to help us take a fresh look at the place we make for learning.

Translating Theory into Practice

How do we translate all we know about space, students, and learning into a master plan for locating, shaping, and using the space called school? While there is obvious danger in being too programmatic about something as dynamic and fluid as alternative learning environments, the following plan for action should result in wise decisions about space:

1. Identify the target population. How many students? What grades? What will they probably be like? What will their special space needs be?

2. Determine the fiscal resources. How much money is there in the budget for facilities, including leasing costs, remodeling, maintenance, and custodial care?

3. Identify the constraints. What do state laws say about school buildings? Are special exceptions made for temporary facilities? What local zoning codes will influence the decision? What fire codes and other local ordinances are important?

4. Select a building search committee. Include on the committee township officials, parents, builders, architects, real estate agents, teachers, and students. Help them develop a systematic plan for identifying all possible spaces for learning. Make up a standard file card to be used for each facility located, with spaces for such information as location, owner, agent, capacity, cost, availability, and parking facilities. Make a tentative list of space needs. On the basis of the number of students and teachers and the nature of the program, develop a specific list of learning space requirements. The following section of this chapter shows an ideal set of space specifications for one hundred students which can be used as a beginning place for a local list.

5. Match space needs with sites available and money obtainable and make a basic decision as to whether all learning activities will be located in one central location, totally decentralized throughout the city, or partially decentralized for certain kinds of learning activities.

6. Get legal advice about making leases that will be to your advantage. Usually it's best—if possible—to get a

ten-month lease, renewable at your option. If the space looks like it is excellent, then try to get a long-term lease if your funds are rather secure.

7. Appoint a committee of staff and students to make tentative decisions about use of space. Make it clear that all space allocations are tentative; no one owns any space as yet—not even the director or his secretary.

8. Let the students and staff use the facilities for several weeks and then make more permanent decisions about the optimal allocation of space.

9. Let students decorate and furnish all the spaces intended primarily for their own use.

10. Every two months evaluate how decisions about space are affecting the program. Try out new arrangements every month; play around with space and observe how new spatial arrangements create new relationships.

What would the result be of weighing all these principles and putting into practice these systematic steps? While there is an obvious danger in trying to propose some ideal allocation of space without regard for site and users, this discussion can be made more specific by an indication of one possible package designed to provide an alternative learning environment for one hundred students and ten adults. (That such a low student–adult ratio is feasible within limited budgets will be demonstrated in the section on staffing.)

At the outset it should be underscored that the spaces listed below can be decentralized; in fact, they might better be seen as space modules that can be assembled into various types of combinations.

1. Business office. There should be a small office, perhaps 200 square feet, with a big sign hanging on the door: "Business Office: No Nonsense Here." Different types of space call for different types of relationships and behavior. Too often the office in the alternative school becomes a hangout where teenager informality and fun make it impossible to get business done efficiently. So the office suggests hardness: bare walls,

hard chairs and desks, bright lights, steel file cabinets, and only one or two chairs for visitors. The office is a place where people use the phone, file reports, keep official records, and leave. And the leaving applies most of all to the director of the alternative school: especially in alternative schools where the director becomes administrator, counselor, public relations man, and general factotum; it becomes too easy for him or her to sit in the office surrounded by suppliants.

2. Seminar rooms. For one hundred students there should be seven seminar rooms, large enough so that fifteen students and one teacher can sit comfortably close. The seminar rooms serve two main purposes. First, they are home base for the counseling groups or tribes—the basic administrative, social, and counseling unit for the school. (The counseling group is described more fully in Chapter 7.) Here students meet one to three times a week for group discussions with their counselor–teacher. The seminar rooms also serve as the primary space for all the discussion-centered learning so important in the core curriculum of the alternative schools. Here groups can meet to discuss modern poetry, civil disobedience, protest movements, creative writing, and ecological principles. Here also seminars in mathematics, foreign languages, and science can be held, when those subjects do not require special equipment or facilities. In a sense these rooms become the basic classrooms in the alternative school.

But their furnishings and their appearance suggest a different feel. They are carpeted, not with heavy-duty institutional carpets, but with whatever colorful rugs and carpets can be scrounged. Hanging at the front of the room is a large pad of newsprint; there are no blackboards. Folding chairs are available when it's time for serious sitting, and floor cushions and mats can quickly be arranged for leisurely discussion. (See the discussion on new furniture at the end of this chapter.) Hanging from the walls (to keep floor space clear) are several bookshelves filled with paperbacks, magazines, and a few basic texts. There is no teacher's desk or file cabinet. No one owns these rooms; they can be used by anyone for informal discussions, private conferences, quiet study, or just relaxing.

No one—neither teachers nor students—may smoke in the seminar rooms; they are too small and their furnishings too flammable.

The counseling groups are encouraged to decorate the seminar rooms where they customarily meet, and are given total freedom as to how they decorate the rooms. Walls can be painted with murals, mobiles can be hung, cushions which the students have made can be brought in, and student art can be hung from the walls.

This one "hard" office and these seven "soft" seminar rooms together can constitute an integrated "home base" for the alternative school, from which students may leave for the rest of their learning activities. All the rest of the units described below can be scattered throughout the community; this core home-base unit will provide enough stability for young people, who need a sense of place. Eriksen (1972), in fact, recommends such a "scattered" school as a good solution for urban alternatives.

3. The community room. This is a room big enough to seat 150. It is used for multiple purposes: weekly town meetings of the student body and staff, evening meetings for parents, indoor games and recreation, dancing, films, listening to music. It is an area of high noise, high physical activity, gross physical movement. Its surfaces are hard, impervious to damage; it is designed to take a hard physical beating. Folding chairs are stacked against the walls. There are several movable platforms which can be pushed together to create a stage. In one corner is a secondhand piano. Against one wall is a quality compact stereo unit resting on top of a lockable cabinet. At the ends of the room basketball backboards have been hung, and movable standards for a volleyball net are at the sides. At the end of the room are a few small folding tables for those who want to play table games in an atmosphere of high noise and movement. A movie screen is permanently fixed on one of the walls, and a locked storage cabinet houses a 16-mm. projector.

The room is in constant use, rarely with any kind of adult

supervision. If anyone wants to claim it for some type of prepared activity—such as a film for a class or a dramatic presentation for the school—he simply signs up on a schedule hung on one of the walls. Reservations are made on a first-come, first-served basis. Regular town meeting time is blocked out in advance; otherwise, anyone may use the space for whatever purpose he or she requires it.

No attempt is made to control the noise or activity level, and no one worries too much about the condition of the room. Here the young people can act like children without being scolded. Since smoking is permitted, there are plenty of sand ash trays and hand fire extinguishers.

4. Center for experimentation. About 600 square feet are needed for this carefully controlled environment to be used for any experimental work in physics, chemistry, biology, psychology, and mathematics. All the surfaces are very hard, impervious to acids and teen-age abuse. Running water, gas, and electric outlets are available for use. Locked cabinets house a few good microscopes, balance beams, pocket calculators, and whatever other basic equipment is required for the experiments. If at all possible, a computer terminal is in one corner. Chemical fire extinguishers are hung from the walls, and good ventilation is provided with a strong exhaust fan. No smoking is allowed.

Adults who know the hard sciences and their experimental techniques are on hand to work with the students, who schedule themselves here for the necessary laboratory work. A few advanced students have small storage cabinets, where their work in progress is safe from tampering. At any given time there might be four students working together on a physics experiment, two students cooperating on a chemistry project, three students experimenting with reaction time in a psychology study, and four students doing a biology experiment together.

The room is quiet and clean. Periodically throughout the day the adults help students do a thorough cleanup of floors, work surfaces, glass, and equipment.

5. The craft center. This is a large room with plenty of natural light. It is used for all crafts requiring heavy machinery and equipment. People work here, alone and in groups, painting, sculpting, carving, sewing, making wood and metal products. Here the subjects of art, home economics, and industrial arts are brought together in a new relationship. This is the place for making and creating objects—and in the process of creating those objects, the distinction between the "fine" and the "practical" arts is obliterated.

The floors and walls are hard because messiness is encouraged. Running water is available. There are a few large workbenches, some easels, a potter's wheel and kiln, a wood lathe, and one or two portable sewing machines. Since there is much flammable material around, no smoking is permitted.

6. The library. This is an old-fashioned word for another "no-nonsense" room, where people read and study quietly. It's a carpeted room with some soft reading chairs around a fireplace. Around the perimeter of the room are carrels, where teachers do their quiet, private work. The room is filled with books and magazines. A file cabinet contains some programmed learning materials and learning packages. A record player and a tape cassette are available—both with earphones, for this is a room where quiet prevails, except for the low hum of conversation between two people. Student artwork decorates the walls. Smoking is permitted at one end of the room and prohibited at the other end.

The room is used for all kinds of quiet thinking and study. Teachers, students, and parents can come in, knowing that there will be quiet and they won't be disturbed. Teachers can use it as the place where they prepare for instruction and do their heavy reading; students can use it for serious study or recreational reading or just quietly thinking and doing nothing. Some quiet talk between two people takes place from time to time, but if the talk gets too animated and noisy, the others in the room put some gentle pressure on the talkers to find another place or reduce the noise level.

7. The kitchen. This is the place where eating, drinking, and smoking flourish. There are vending machines for bever-

ages, candy, and sandwiches. There are four small round tables big enough to seat six, for at no time will there be more than perhaps twenty-five people in the room. It will be a messy place, so all the surfaces are easily cleanable. There is a refrigerator against one wall for those who want to store their yogurt, raw vegetables, fruit juice, and fruit—staples now in the diets of many young people. There is a small electric range, where anyone can heat some soup or make a cake. Around the lunch hour one of the teachers who likes to cook meets with boys and girls who want to learn how to improve their cooking and create new dishes.

A small FM radio plays quietly; those who want to listen to loud rock move to the assembly room. This is a place where young and old can eat and drink and smoke (if they choose) and talk quietly. It should have the feel of the old family kitchen, where good food and fresh coffee made it easy to relax and talk.

8. The communications center. This is the message center of the school—the place where all the words are churned out. There are typewriters, a copying machine, duplicating and mimeograph machines, possibly a small printing press, telephones, large bulletin boards, and mailboxes for everyone. This is the place where students publish their own newspaper and magazines, where teachers run off materials for class, where course catalogs are published, where newsletters to parents are prepared. If at all possible, a large closet is equipped as a dark room.

9. The meditation room. This is a very small room, perhaps less than a hundred square feet in area. It is just big enough for one or two people, certainly no more than three. The floor is covered entirely with mats. The walls are bare, painted white. There are a few prayer cushions on the floor. On a corner shelf are nine or ten books on prayer and meditation. There is a small low table. And on a shelf on one of the walls are symbols, objects, and aids to meditation from the various religions, so that as the person enters, he may quickly arrange his own private altar if he wants one.

The rule is absolute silence, so that everyone knows he may sit there in the quiet without being disturbed by questions or casual greetings. People leave their shoes at the door as they enter. Two signs have been prepared to hang on the corridor side of the door. One reads, "Please wait outside; I prefer to be alone for a little while." The other reads, "Enter quietly if you wish."

This is the place where one can cry and not feel ashamed, lie down and not feel sinful, pray and not feel embarrassed, do nothing and not feel guilty.

10. The grounds outside. There is a parking lot for thirty cars, with a basketball backboard and hoop. There are a flower garden and a small organic vegetable garden. There are a few benches where people can sit and talk.

Obviously, such an aggregate of space is ideal; in any real setting compromises will have to be made, and space will have to serve double purposes. The intent, however, has been to describe a kind of human, not architectural, ideal, responsive to teen-agers as they really are, not as we think they ought to be. Let us highlight at the end here the essential goals which this alternative learning environment has tried to achieve:

1. We begin by looking at learning, not subjects. We forget about home economics and ask instead, "Do we need a place where people can sew? Do we need a place where people can cook and eat together?" And we find new relationships—so that dance and theater and film and gym go together, and sewing and woodworking and painting share space.

2. We look at the ways in which people—young and old alike—spend their time alone and in groups. We make some places designed for one or two, some for cliques of ten, some for crowds of thirty, and some for mobs of one hundred.

3. We design places for people and activities regardless of status. There are no separate faculty lunchrooms and student toilets, but each person is able to find quiet and privacy when he or she needs it.

4. We furnish and equip these spaces quite differently.

Some are hard and almost sterile. Some are soft and almost plush. The environment is created in order to facilitate the kind of behavior we think will occur in those special places.

5. We establish zones of noise. In one place there is absolute quiet so that one can hear the silence. In a few places quiet talk and soft music are heard. And in a few places we expect a high noise level—loud music, dancing, yelling, cheering.

6. We permit different levels of cleanliness. In the meditation room and in the experimentation room, we demand absolute cleanliness. In the craft room, the kitchen, and the assembly room, we expect some messiness. In the seminar rooms we expect a tolerable level of human disorder.

7. We permit smoking in some areas and not in others —not capriciously, but logically on the basis of the activity taking place and the fire hazards prevailing. And the same rules apply to everyone—students, teachers, visitors, and parents alike.

8. We discriminate between the amount of nonsense encouraged and allowed. Anyone who eats, plays a radio, and lounges on the desk in the office is in for trouble, and anyone who tries to look solemn and businesslike in the assembly room is out of place.

There is a lesson here for the staff members of conventional schools who feel they are stuck with unimaginative and traditional buildings. The lesson is the need to differentiate space in terms of human needs. Any staff, along with interested students, can survey its building and decide which of these places of the alternative environment can be made to fit in the conventional building.

A Closing Note About School Furniture

As you may have noted, all of the conventional school furniture has been left out of the environment described above. Almost all school furniture, even the most modern, is badly designed for human beings, and it reminds the students of the institutional living they have tried to put behind them. Perhaps it is time for all of us to stop buying school furniture and think more creatively about the kind of furniture people need in order to learn and work together. We would not only produce a more human environment, but we would also effect a substantial savings. So for any learning environment—alternative or not—what we really need is:

> small circular tables to seat six to eight workbenches
> plenty of folding chairs, half with tablet arms
> movable platforms that can be stacked
> pads of newsprint which can be easily attached to the walls
> several soft chairs and sofas, sturdily constructed
> floor cushions
> several study carrels
> boxes and cubes that can be used for sitting, stacking, playing
> foam mats
> removable display boards

And wherever possible, of course, students should be deeply involved in buying, scrounging, making, and painting the furniture they are using.

References

Coleman, James S. *The Adolescent Society*. New York: Free Press, 1961.

Dunphy, D. C. "The Social Structure of Urban Adolescent Peer Groups," *Sociometry*, 26 (1963), pp. 230–246.

Eriksen, Aase. *Scattered Schools*. New York: Educational Facilities Laboratory, 1972.

Eriksen, Aase. "Space for Learning," *NASSP Bulletin*, No. 374 (September 1973).

Goffman, Erving. *Relations in Public*. New York: Basic Books, 1971.

Hall, Edward T. *The Hidden Dimension*. Garden City, New York: Doubleday, 1966.

Holt, John. *Freedom and Beyond*. New York: Dutton, 1972.

Illich, Ivan. *De-schooling Society*. New York: Harper and Row, 1971.

Lang, Jon. "Architecture of Human Behavior: The Nature of the Problem," *Architecture of Human Behavior*. Philadelphia: AIA, 1971.

Luce, Gay G. *Body Time*. New York: Pantheon Books, 1971.

"Places and Things for Experimental Schools." New York: Educational Facilities Laboratories, 1972.

Somer, Robert. *Personal Space: The Behavioral Basis of Design*. Englewood Cliffs, New Jersey: Prentice-Hall, 1969.

A Concluding Note

The big schools, public and parochial, are not prisons staffed with mindless guards. They are changing institutions, staffed with competent and conscientious teachers doing their damnedest in difficult times to teach young people. And for close to two-thirds of these young people, the big schools seem to be working with some measure of success. The author wishes those schools well and praises those teachers for their commitment and concern.

But for those teachers and those young people who are dissatisfied, the author thinks alternatives can provide a better way. And the better way is not a trickier schedule or a slicker curriculum or a fancier gym. It is, instead, a chance to build a community—to create a place where people can live and work together in an atmosphere of trust, in a climate of hope.

The author does not know what will happen to the alternative school movement. He senses it will continue to grow until it too has become institutionalized, and then ultimately, it will die. But it will have made an impact. And for hundreds of us, it will have given us a chance to come alive again, to give birth to our vision, to touch a life. We will have pretended we made those schools for the young. All the time it was for our own salvation.

Bibliography

Books

Adams, Don, with Gerald Reagan. *Schooling and Social Change in Modern America*. New York: David McKay, 1972.

Arons, Stephen, et al. *Alternative Schools: A Practical Manual*. Cambridge, Massachusetts: Center for Law and Education, Harvard University, 1971.

Barth, Roland S. *Open Education and the American School*. New York: Agathon Press, 1972.

Bhaerman, Robert (ed.). *Quest '72: A Look at Alternative Schools*. Resource Notebook, AFT-Quest Convention Program, Washington, D.C., 1972.

Bremer, John, and Michael von Moschzisker. *The School Without Walls: Philadelphia's Parkway Program*. New York: Holt, Rinehart, and Winston, 1971.

Brown, Frank. *The Non Graded High School*. Englewood Cliffs, New Jersey: Prentice-Hall, 1963.

Cox, Donald. *The City As Schoolhouse: The Story of the Parkway Program*. Valley Forge, Pennsylvania: Judson Press, 1972.

Dennison, George. *The Lives of Children: The Story of the First Street School*. New York: Random House, 1969.

Eriksen, Aase. *Scattered School*, Report, University of Pennsylvania, U.S. Department of Health, Education, and Welfare, 1971.

Fantini, Mario D., and Gerald Weinstein. *The Disadvantaged: Challenge to Education*. New York: Harper and Row, 1968.

Fantini, Mario D. *Public Schools of Choice*. New York: Simon and Schuster, 1974.

Freire, Paulo, *Pedagogy of the Oppressed*. New York: Herder and Herder, 1970.

French, William Marshall. *American Secondary Education*. 2nd ed. New York: Odyssey Press, 1967.

Glines, Don. *Creating Human Schools*. Revised. Mankato, Minnesota: Campus Publishers, 1972.

Graubard, Allen. *Free the Children: Radical Reform and the Free School Movement*. New York: Pantheon Books, 1972.

Great Atlantic and Pacific School Conspiracy, The, *Doing Your Own School: A Practical Guide to Starting and Operating A Community School*. Boston: Beacon Press, 1972.

Gross, Ronald, and Beatrice Gross (eds.). *Radical School Reform*. New York: Simon and Schuster, 1970.

Gross, Ronald, and Paul Osterman (eds.). *High School*. New York: Simon and Schuster, 1971.

Hassett, Joseph, and Arline Weisberg. *Open Education: Alternatives Within Our Tradition*. Englewood Cliffs, New Jersey: Prentice-Hall, 1972.

225

Herndon, James. *How to Survive in Your Native Land*. New York: Simon and Schuster, 1971.

Holt, John. *How Children Learn*. New York: Pitman, 1967.

Kohl, Herbert. *The Open Classroom*. New York: Random House, 1969.

Kozol, Jonathan. *Free Schools*. Boston: Houghton Mifflin, 1972.

Moody, Charles D., Charles B. Vergon, and Jean Leonard (eds.). *Alternative Education in a Pluralistic Society*. Ann Arbor: University of Michigan Press, 1973.

Moore, Donald R., et al. *The Metro School: A Report on the Progress of Chicago's Experimental School Without Walls*. Chicago: Urban Research Corporation, 1971.

Nyquist, Ewald, and Gene Hawes. *Open Education: A Sourcebook for Parents and Teachers*. New York: Bantam, 1972.

Perrone, Vito. *Open Education: Promise and Problems*. Bloomington, Indiana: Phi Delta Books, 1971, pp. 12–13.

Places and Things for Experimental Schools. Educational Facilities Laboratories (and Experimental Schools Program, U.S.O.E.) New York, 1972.

Postman, Neil, and Charles Weingartner. *The Soft Revolution*. New York: Delta Books, 1971, pp. 12–13.

President's Commission on School Finance. *Final Report*. Washington, D.C.: U.S. Government Printing Office, 1972, p. 76.

Rasberry, Salli, and Robert Greenway. *Rasberry Exercises: How to Start Your Own School and Make a Book*. Freestone, California: Freestone Publishing, 1970.

Reimer, Everett. *School Is Dead*. Garden City, New York: Doubleday, 1971.

Rist, Ray. *Reconstructing American Education: Innovation and Alternatives*. New Brunswick, New Jersey: Transaction Books, 1972, p. 281.

Rogers, Vincent. *Teaching in the British Primary Schools*. New York: Macmillian, 1970.

Rothman, Esther. *The Angel Inside Went Sour*. New York: Bantam, 1970.

Saxe, Richard W. (ed.). *Opening the Schools: Alternative Ways of Learning*. Berkeley, California: McCutchan Publishing, 1972.

Silberman, Charles E. *Crisis in the Classroom: The Remaking of American Education*. New York: Random House, 1970.

Sizer, Theodore R. *Places for Learning, Places for Joy: Speculation on American School Reform*. Cambridge, Massachusetts: Harvard University Press, 1973.

Student Involvement in Decision Making in an Alternative High School. Chicago: Center for New Schools, 1971.

Periodicals and Monographs

"All About Alternatives," *Nation's Schools*, November 1972.

Allen, Dwight. "Alternative Public Schools for the Future," *Individualized Education*, Minneapolis School Facilities Council, 1971, pp. 17–32.

"Alternative High Schools: Some Pioneer Programs," Educational Research Service Circular No. 4, Washington, D.C.: NEA Research Division Educational Research Services, 1972, p. 55.

Alternative Schools: A Practical Manual. Harvard Center for Law and Education, 24 Garden Street, Cambridge, Massachusetts.

"Alternative Schools: Pioneering Districts Create Options for Students," Arlington, Virginia: National School Public Relations Association, 1973.

"Alternative to Public School Is Public School, The," *Observations From the Treadmill*, May 1972, pp. 1–14.

"Alternatives to Tradition," *Education Yearbook*. New York: Free Press, 1973–1974.

Armstrong, D. G. "Alternative Schools: Implications for Secondary School Curriculum Workers," *High School Journal*, 56 (March 1973), pp. 267–386.

Arons, Stephen. "Equity, Options, and Vouchers," *Teacher College Record*, 72 (February 1971), pp. 337–363.

Bainis, J., and William Young. "Sudden Rise and Decline of New Jersey Street Academies," *Phi Delta Kappan*, 53 (December 1971), pp, 200–201.

Barr, Robert D. "The Age of Alternatives: A Developing Trend in Educational Reform," *Changing Schools*, No. 1, pp. 1–3.

Barr, Robert D., Daniel Burke, and Vernon Smith. "All About Alternatives," *Nation's Schools*, Vol. 90, No. 5 (November 1972), pp. 33–39.

Bhaerman, Robert. "Assessing the Alternative Schools," *American Teacher* (June 1972), p. 12.

Blackman, Nathaniel. "Metro: Experimental High School Without Walls, Chicago," *National Association Secondary School Principals Bulletin*, 55 (May 1971), pp. 147–150.

Blackman, Nathaniel. "Observations on One Alternative: Metro High," Chapter 28 in *Opening The Schools*, edited by Richard W. Saxe. Berkeley, California: McCutchan Publishing, 1972.

Bock, Frederick S., and Wanda Gomula. "A Conservative Community Forms an Alternative High School," *Phi Delta Kappan*, 94 (March 1973).

Broudy, Harry S. "Educational Alternatives—Why? Why Not?" *Phi Delta Kappan*, 54 (March 1973).

Brownson, Bill. "Alternative Schools and the Problem of Change: School Is a School Is a School . . ." *Contemporary Education*, Vol. 44, No. 4 (April 1973).

Burke, Daniel. "Alternative Educational Strategies," *Pennsylvania Schoolmaster* (April 1972) pp. 20–21.

Capron, Barbara, Stanley Kluman, and Tedd Levy. "Alternative Schools: Agents for Change?" *SSEC Newsletter* (May 1972), pp. 1–6.

Cass, James. "Beloit-Turner: A School Designed for Kids," *Saturday Review*, March 21, 1970, pp. 65–69.

Center for New Schools. "Strengthening Alternative High School," *Harvard Educational Review*, 42 (August 1972), pp. 313–350.

Changing Schools. National Consortium for Options in Public Education, Bloomington: Indiana University.

Clark, Kenneth. "Alternative Schools," in *High School 1980*, edited by Alvin C. Eurich. New York, Pitman Publishing Co., 1970, pp. 89–102.

Clayton, A. Stafford. "Vital Questions, Minimal Responses: Education Vouchers," *Phi Delta Kappan* (September 1970), pp. 53–54.

Coleman, James S. "The Children Have Outgrown the Schools," *National Elementary Principal*, October 1972.

Coleman, James S. "Class Integration: A Fundamental Break with the Past," *Saturday Review*, May 27, 1972, pp. 58–59.

Cooper, Bruce S. "Free and Freedom Schools: A National Survey of Alternative Programs," A Report to the President's Commission on School Finance, November 1971.

Cooper, Bruce S. "Organizational Survivals, A Comparative Case of Seven American 'Free Schools,'" *Education and Urban Society*, Vol. 5, No. 4 (August 1973).

DeTurk, Philip, and Robert Mackin. "Lions in the Park: An Alternative Meaning and Setting for Learning," *Phi Delta Kappan*, 54 (March 1973) pp. 458–460.

Divoky, Diane. "Berkeley's Experimental Schools," *Saturday Review*, 55 (October 1972).

Dobbins, Alan. "Instruction at Adams," *Phi Delta Kappan*, 52 (May 1971).

Doll, Ronald. "Alternative Forms of Schooling," *Educational Leadership* (February 1972), pp. 391–393.

Doll, R. C., et al. "Systems Renewal in a Big City School District, the Lessons of Louisville," *Phi Delta Kappan*, 54, 8 (April 1973), pp. 524–534.

Educational Leadership. February, 1972 (Issue's theme: Alternative Forms of Schooling).

Edwards, Conan S. "Developing Alternatives in Education," *NASSP Bulletin*, 56 (May 1972).

Eriksen, Aase, and Joseph Gantz. "Business in Public Education," *Wharton Quarterly* (Summer 1971), pp. 11–16.

Ericksen, Aase, and Judith Messina. "The Dynamics of Leadership in an Informal School," *Journal of Research and Development in Education*, 5 (Spring 1972), pp. 29–39.

Erickson, Donald A., and John D. Donovan. "The Three R's of Nonpublic Education," in *Louisiana: Race, Religion, and Region*. A Report to the President's Commission on School Finance. Chicago, 1972.

"Experiment in Free Form Education, An," *Ohio Schools* (April 10, 1970), p. 30.

"Experimental Schools Program," *Nation's Schools*, 88 (September 1971), pp. 56–58.

Fantini, Mario. "Alternative Patterns of Community Participation in Public Education," *Minnesota Education*, 1 (Spring 1973), pp. 13–20.

Fantini, Mario. "Alternatives Within Public Schools," *Phi Delta Kappan*, 55 (March 1973), pp. 444–448.

Fantini, Mario. "Educational Agenda for the 1970's and Beyond: Public Schools of Choice" (with introduction by Alan Gartner), *Social Policy* (November/December 1970), pp. 24–31.

Fantini, Mario. "Options for Students, Parents, and Teachers: Public Schools of Choice," *Phi Delta Kappan*, 52 (May 1971), pp. 541–543.

Fantini, Mario. "Public Schools of Choice and the Plurality of Publics," *Educational Leadership* (March 1971), pp. 585–591.

Fantini, Mario. "Rocket Age—Rickety Curriculum: Public Schools of Choice," *PTA Magazine* (January 1971), pp. 1–4.

Fantini, Mario. "The What, Why, and Where of the Alternative Movement," *National Elementary Principal* (April 1973), pp. 14–22.

Finkelstein, Leonard. "The Parkway Program Evaluation: The Director's Perspective," *Changing Schools*, No. 6, 1973, pp. 16–19.

Finkelstein, Leonard. "The Philadelphia Story," *National Elementary Principal*, 52 (April 1973), pp. 99–101.

Glatthorn, Allan A., and Vernon H. Smith. "More Options: Alternatives to Conventional School," Curriculum Report, *NASSP Bulletin* (March 1973).

Glatthorn, Allan A., and Jon Briskin. "Schools on Wheels: Alternative School Project, Philadelphia." *Today's Education* 62 (May 1973).

"Great Alternatives Hassle, The," *National Elementary Principal*, 52 (April 1973).

Greenberg, James D., and Robert E. Roush. "A Visit to the 'School Without Walls': Two Impressions," *Phi Delta Kappan*, 51 (May 1970).

Gross, Ronald. "From Innovations to Alternatives: A Decade of Change in Education," *Phi Delta Kappan*, 52 (September 1971), pp. 22–24.

Guernsey, John. "Portland's Unconventional Adams High," *American Education*, 6 (May 1970).

Harvard Educational Review, Vol. 42, No. 3 (August 1972).

Haugh, Richard F. "Education by Choice," Quincy School District, Quincy, Ill., 1974.

Havighurst, Robert. "The Unknown Good: Education Vouchers," *Phi Delta Kappan*, 52 (September 1970), pp. 52–53.

Hickey, Mike. "Alternative Education, Seattle," Seattle (Washington) School District, 1972.

Hickey, Mike. "Alternative Education and Public Schools: Is Peaceful Cohabitation Possible?" *Changing Schools*, No. 3, 1972, pp. 1–5.

Hickey, Mike. *Evaluating Alternative Schools*. Position Paper, National Consortium for Options in Public Education, 1972, 7 pp.

Holton, C. K. "Challenge of Change: Roles and Relationships, Woodlawn Experimental Schools Project," *Educational Leadership*, 29 (February 1972), pp. 391–393.

Howes, Kimball L. "Reaching the 'Tuned Out' Student on His Own Terms," *Ohio Schools*, 64 (November 16, 1971), pp. 20–21.

Hutchins, Robert M. "The Great Anti-School Campaign," *The Great Ideas Today*. Chicago: Encyclopaedia Britannica, 1972.

Illich, Ivan. "The Alternatives to Schooling," *Saturday Review*, June 1971, pp. 44–48.

Janssen, Peter A. "Skyline: The School with Something for Everyone," *Saturday Review*, December 1972.

Jencks, Christopher. "Giving Parents Money for Schooling: Education Vouchers," *Phi Delta Kappan*, 52 (September 1970), pp. 49–52.

Jenkins, Evans. "Community Life: Schools Become the Host for Public Services," *The New York Times*, December 23, 1973.

Johnston, David. "Strategies in Developing and Implementing an Alternative School," *Two Case Studies*, Position Paper, National Consortium for Options in Public Education, 1972, pp. 11–17.

Kammann, Richard. "The Case for Making Each School in Your District 'Different'—and Letting Parents Choose the One Best for Their Child," *The American School Board Journal* (January 1972), pp. 37–38.

Katz, Malcolm. "Educational Pluralism for Local School Districts," *MASB Journal* (December 1971), pp. 26–29.

Kohl, Herbert. "What Are the Real Risks When a School Tries to Change?" *Saturday Review*, May 27, 1972, pp. 50–54.

Kohn, Sherwood. "Getting Attention in California," *National Elementary Principal*, 52 (April 1973), pp. 90–98.

Kozol, Jonathan. "Free Schools," *The Boston Globe*, Sunday Magazine, March 12, 1972, pp. 4–5, 12–13.

Kozol, Jonathan. "Free Schools: A Time for Candor," *Saturday Review*, March 4, 1972.

Levine, C. "John Dewey School Adventure," *Phi Delta Kappan*, 53 (October 1971), p. 105.

Lewis, B. R. "Innovative High School in a Midwestern Suburb," *Phi Delta Kappan*, 53 (October 1971), p. 105.

Lydiard, Beverly, and Beverly Simon. *Kaleidoscope*. Boston: Massachusetts Department of Education, 1973.

McCarthy, Robert, and Thomas Hanlon. "Critical Factors in Planning an Alternative School Program," *Planning and Implementing Alternative Public Schools: Two Case Studies*. Position paper, National Consortium for Options in Public Education, 1972, pp. 1–10.

McClintock, Robert. "Universal Voluntary Study," *The Center Magazine* (January/February 1973), pp. 24–30.

McPherson, R. Bruce, et al. "Options for Students in Ann Arbor," *Phi Delta Kappan*, 54 (March 1973), pp. 469–470.

Morford, John A., and Sally H. Wertheim. *Alternative Schools in Greater Cleveland*. Martha Holden Jennings Foundation, Cleveland, 1973.

Morse, David. "The Alternatives," *Media and Methods*, 7 (May 1971), pp. 29–34, 63–64.

Murray, H. G. "Students Drop In, Not Out: Lynchburg Learning Center, Virginia," *Clearing House*, 46 (January 1972), p. 300.

NASSP Bulletin, Vol. 57, No. 374, (September 1973).

"Need for Alternative Schools Within the Public School System," *School Management*, 17 (April 1973), pp. 8–9.

New Schools Exchange Newsletter, 30 W. Cota, Santa Barbara, California, 93101.

Parker, John L. "Teacher Training at Adams," *Phi Delta Kappan* 52 (May 1971).

Patton, William, and Robert A. Anderson. "Educational Vouchers for the Community?" *Theory into Practice*, 11 (February 1972).

Perron, Jack. "Alternative Publishing and Education," *Phi Delta Kappan*, 54 (March 1973), pp. 461–464.

Postman, Neil. "Alternative Education in the Seventies," last supplement to *Whole Earth Catalog*.

Pugh, Nathaniel, Jr. "The Human Element in Alternative Education," *NASSP Bulletin*, 52 (May 1972).

Render, Gary, Charles E. Moon, and Donald J. Treffinger. "Directory of Organization and Periodicals on Alternative Education," *The Journal of Creative Behavior*, 7 (1973), pp. 53–66.

Resnick, Henry. "Promise of Change in North Dakota," *Saturday Review*, April 17, 1971, pp. 67–69, 79–88.

Riordan, Robert. "Alternative Schools in Action; Bloomington, Indiana," Phi Delta Kappa Educational Foundation, 1972.

Robinson, Donald. "Alternative Schools: Challenge to Traditional Education?" *Phi Delta Kappan* (March 1970), pp. 374–375.

Robinson, Donald. "Alternative Schools—Do They Promise System Reform?" *Phi Delta Kappan*, (March 1973), pp. 433, 443.

Robinson Donald. "Alternative Schools: Is the Older Order Really Changing?" *Educational Leadership* (March 1971), pp. 604–607.

Robinson, Donald. "Legitimizing the Revolution," *Phi Delta Kappan*, 53 (February 1973), p. 400.

Rosen, David. "New Evaluation for New Schools," *Changing Schools*, No. 6, 1973, pp. 3–15, 23.

Roth Virginia. "A Model for an Alternative High School, Austin, Texas," Austin Writers Group, 1973.

Saxe, Richard. "Can We Have Alternatives and Schools Too?" *National Elementary Principal*, 52 (April 1973), pp. 102–104.

"Schools with a Difference," *Newsweek*, April 23, 1973, pp. 113–116.

Shave, H. G. "Innovation: An Ongoing Process," *Educational Leadership*, 30 (March 1973), pp. 507–509.

Singleton, Steven, David Boyer, and Paul Dorsey. "Xanadu: A Study of the Structure Crisis in an Alternative School," *Review of Educational Research*, Vol. 42, No. 4 (Fall 1972).

Smith, Mortimer. "CBE Views the Alternatives," *Phi Delta Kappan*, 54 (March 1973).

Smith, Vernon. "Options in Public Education: The Quiet Revolution," *Phi Delta Kappan*, 54 (March 1973), pp. 434–437.

Stansfield, David. "The Importance of Being Different: The Case for Diversity in Education," *Media and Methods* (April 1971), pp. 33–36.

"Students Writing About Their Experiences in Alternative Public Schools," *Changing Schools*, No. 5, 1973.

Teacher Paper, The 2221 N. E. 23rd Street, Portland, Oregon, 97212.

This Magazine Is About Schools, 56 Esplanade Street, Toronto, Ontario, Canada.

"Title III and Changing Educational Designs," National Advisory Council on Supplementary Centers and Services, Washington, D.C., George Washington University, 1973.

Walker, Penelope (ed.). "Public Alternative Schools: A Look at the Options," Amherst, Massachusetts, National Alternative Schools Program, 1973.

Wertheim, Sally H., and William P. Hoffman. "Alternative Programs in Public Secondary Schools in Greater Cleveland: A Descriptive Study," Martha Holden Jennings Foundation, Cleveland, 1974.

Wertheimer, Patricia. "School Climate and School Learning," *Phi Delta Kappan*, 52 (May 1971), pp. 518–530.

White House Conference on Children, Report to the President. Washington, D.C., U.S. Government Printing Office, 1970, p. 423.

Yarger, Sam. "Why Alternatives," in *Opening the Schools* edited by Richard W. Saxe. Berkeley, California: McCutchan Publishing, 1972, pp. 66–83.

Resource Centers

Center for New Schools, 431 South Dearborn, Suite 1527, Chicago, Illinois, 60605.

Educational Exploration Center, 3104 16th Avenue South, Minneapolis, Minnesota, 55407.

Gemini Institute, Consultants for Experimental Education Programs, 8162 Sycamore, Indianapolis, Indiana, 47240.

International Consortium for Options in Public Education, The, School of Education, Indiana University, Bloomington, Indiana, 47401.

Learning Center, c/o Exploring Family School, Box 1442, El Cajon, California, 92021.

National Alternative Schools Program (NASP), School of Education, University of Massachusetts, Amherst, Massachusetts, 01002.

New Schools Exchange, 301 East Canon Perdido, Santa Barbara, California, 93101.

New Schools Movement, 117 Madrone Place East, Seattle, Washington, 98102.

Teacher Drop-Out Center, The, Box 521, Amherst, Massachusetts, 01002.

Index